MIND

&

MOTIVATION

MIND

&

MOTIVATION

Reconnecting with Your Inner Purpose

Lisa Tenzin-Dolma

Published by Phoenix Rising Press 2019

MIND & MOTIVATION

2nd Edition
1st Edition published by Phoenix Rising Press 2008

ISBN 978-1-916-21530-6

Contents

Other Books
By The Author

Emotional Healing for Dogs: Combining Bach Flower Remedies and Behaviour Therapy
The 'Supposedly' Enlightened Person's Guide to Raising a Dog (with Kac Young)
Charlie, the Dog Who Came in From the Wild
Lainey Lainey (fiction)
Lainey's Lot (fiction)
The Swan Lake (fiction)
The Heartbeat at Your Feet: A Practical, Compassionate New Way to Train Your Dog
Dog Training: The Essential Guide (also the updated 2nd edition, The Essential Guide to Dog Training)
Adopting a Rescue Dog
The Mindful Mandala Colouring Book
Mandala Source Book (with David Fontana)
Natural Mandalas
Healing Mandalas
The Mandala Colouring Kit
The Celtic Mandala Colouring Kit
Celtic Mandalas Colouring Book
Buddhist Mandalas Colouring Book
Buddhist Pocket Mandala Colouring Book
Healing Mandalas Colouring Book
The Healing Mandala Pocket Colouring Book

The Celtic Mandala Colouring Kit
3D Mandalas
Take Control with Astrology
Teach Yourself Astrology
Understanding the Planetary Myths
A-Z of Dreaming
Understanding Your Dreams
Dreams & Dreaming
The Glastonbury Tarot textbook
The Glastonbury Tarot, revised edition
The Glastonbury Tarot, 1st edition
Swimming with Dolphins
The Dolphin Experience
Further information about Lisa Tenzin-Dolma and her books can be found at http://www.tenzindolma.co.uk

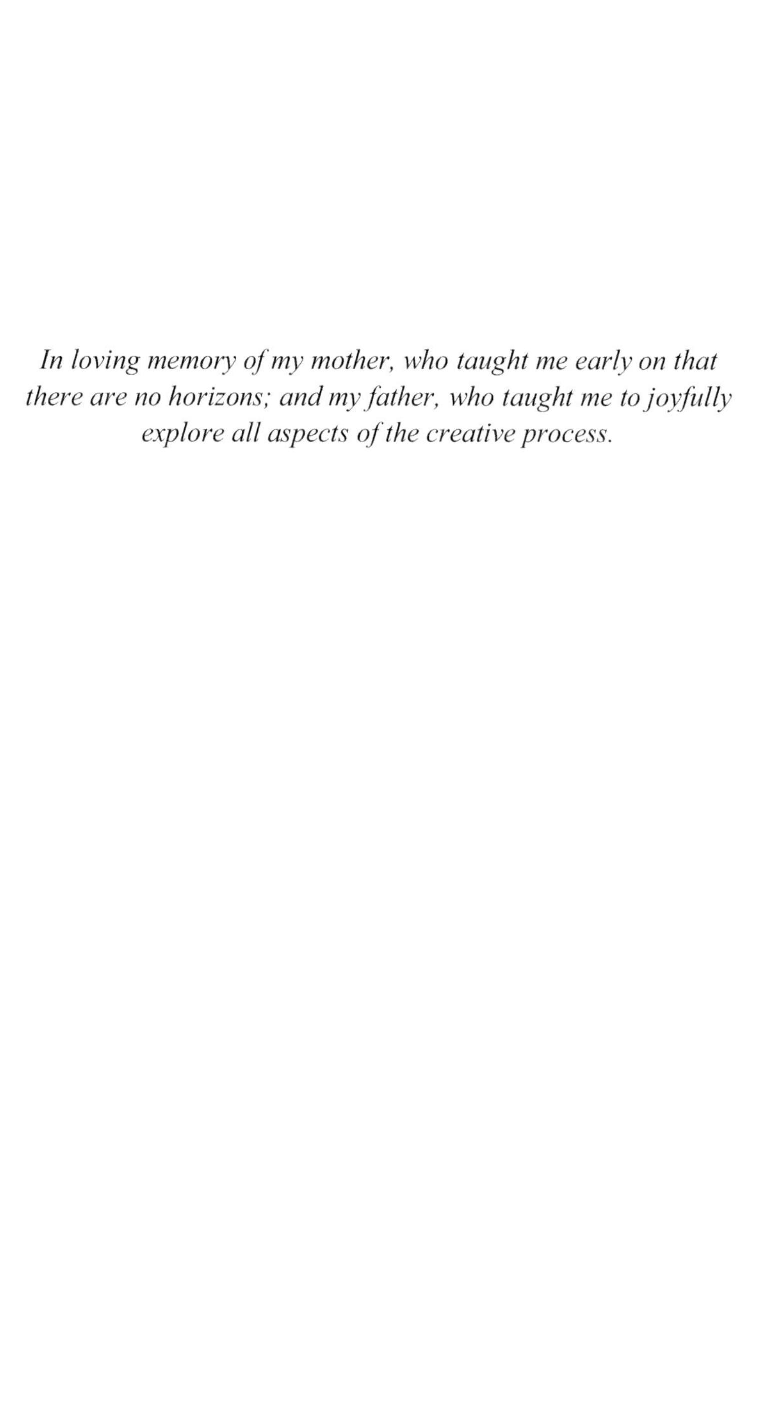

In loving memory of my mother, who taught me early on that there are no horizons; and my father, who taught me to joyfully explore all aspects of the creative process.

About The Author

Lisa Tenzin-Dolma is the author of 34 books and hundreds of articles. Since childhood she has been fascinated by what makes us who we are, and how we can tap into various aspects of the self to fulfil our true potential.

She has worked as a musician, songwriter, nurse, counsellor, holistic therapist, clothes and jewellery designer, wholefood cook, journalist, artist and illustrator, medical laboratory assistant, and canine behaviourist. Her deep love for dogs led her to train as a canine psychologist and behaviourist, and Lisa founded The International School for Canine Psychology & Behaviour Ltd., The Dog Welfare Alliance, and she is a co-founder of ICAN, the International Companion Animal Network. She writes monthly features about dog emotions and new scientific studies for Edition Dog Magazine. Lisa lives in Bath, UK.

Acknowledgements

Many thanks to Peter Russell, Michael Eavis, Willard Wigan MBE, Peter Ulrich, Dr. Sam Parnia, Colin Wilson, Dr. Jean Houston, Dr. Natalie Rogers and Joanne Harris were generous about sharing their experiences and wisdom for the interviews at the conclusion of each chapter. These are all people whose lives and work have made a lasting impact on my life, and whose work has spread ripples across the world and helped to change the way we view ourselves, life and the world. Their openness, warmth and honesty is truly heart-warming. Sadly, Colin and Natalie have since passed away and will be much missed by countless people who were nurtured and uplifted by their extraordinary, life-enhancing work. I feel privileged to have had the opportunity to speak with them and to record our conversations for their interviews. Thank you to Dr. Frances Fuchs, Natalie's daughter, for permission from the Rogers Trust to include my interview with Natalie.

Hugs and massive thanks to Dr. Paul Halpern for writing the Foreword for this book, and for being a constant source of motivation and inspiration throughout the years of our friendship. Paul's compelling popular science books give tremendous insights into the nature of the universe, and into the personalities of some of the extraordinary minds who have made astonishing discoveries in physics and cosmology.

NASA, ESA, T. Megeath (University of Toledo) and M. Robberto (STScl) graciously gave permission for the use of the beautiful Hubble Telescope image of the Orion Nebula for the book cover. Thank you to all, and thanks also to STScl for adding a copy of *Mind & Motivation* to their archives.

My children, Ryan, Oliver, Daniel, Liam and Amber are the true treasures of my life, and I feel privileged to have grown with them while I have watched them grow up. Their partners, Kelly, Carrie, Hema, Courtney and Sam are sources of great joy, and so is Lara, my beautiful granddaughter. My late mother, Betty, instilled in me from an early age the understanding that there are no horizons, and that the only limitations to curiosity and self-knowledge are those that we create for ourselves. My late father, Harold, showed me the delights of being focused on the creative process. My sister and dearest friend, Julie Gutteridge, is always a shining example to me of what can be achieved when you have the will and determination, and a wicked sense of humour.

Friends are such a precious gift. Love and thanks to Sarah Fisher; Paul and Felicia Hurewitz; my cousin Sue Beech; Annie and Bryan Rawlings; Andrew and Kieron Hale; Jen Govey; Carole Cox; Yolanda Scott; Caroline Wilkinson and Jon Holloway; Michael Eastwood and Marius Von Brasch; Dale McLelland, June Pennell, Teresa Tyler, Theo Stewart and all my wonderful team-mates at The International School for Canine Psychology & Behaviour Ltd. Huge thanks (and, I promise, regular boxes of Jaffa Cakes) to Sam Jellyman for the conversational boost I needed to complete this book in a burst of energy and enthusiasm.

And, last but definitely not least, thank you to each of you, dear readers, for doing me the honour of reading this book. I hope you've enjoyed it!

Summary
Of The Chapters

INTRODUCTION

The aim of this book - to encourage the unfolding of potential which enables you to feel an increased sense of fulfilment and purpose.

PATHWORKING EXERCISE

CHAPTER 1. A SENSE OF PURPOSE

Purpose, and the tapestry of life. What makes you feel fulfilled? Life as a journey of discovery. Choice. The clustering effect. Unconscious patterns. Looking back to what has given you the greatest pleasure and carrying that feeling forward into the present time. Taking notice of coincidences and synchronicity. Evaluating what you enjoy doing and are good at. Moving forward. Setting goals. Connecting with other people. Noticing what energises you and creates a sense of 'rightness'. Higher purpose: fulfilling the spiritual as well as emotional and material aspects of life.

Peter Russell. Author of eight books on science and consciousness. Film-maker, scientist and psychologist. Peter's research into the psychology of meditation has been instrumental in the consciousness revolution, and the increasing integration of science and metaphysics. Peter's interview is a thought-provoking combination of wisdom and deep scientific knowledge.

CHAPTER 2. MOTIVATION

The instinctive life-urge. The creative force. The drive to direct energy towards a specific goal or purpose. Being clear about what you want to achieve. What makes one person more motivated than another? A sense of direction. Focus, discipline, energy, enthusiasm, confidence, one-pointedness, rebellion, determination. The ability to stand alone and believe in yourself - but also to communicate ideas effectively to others. A motive - a reason; motivate - to move forward. Looking at whether your motivation is fear-based or love-based. How wrong motivation has brought about the global crisis; how correct motivation enables us to function at a higher harmonic and fulfil our purpose in life.

Michael Eavis. The Founder and organiser of the world-famous Glastonbury Festival of Performing Arts. Michael talks about how the love-based impetus that brought about the first Glastonbury Festival, describes what motivates him, and offers suggestions that will help to add impetus to ideas.

CHAPTER 3. DEALING WITH CHALLENGES

The ability to face up to, deal with, and overcome challenges and obstacles. How what seems like 'failure' can open up new areas of thought and ideas, which lead to success. Recognising that and finding fresh avenues of exploration. Challenges and the growth process. The story of Percival and the Fisher King as an illustration of apparent failure that led to wisdom, and eventual accomplishment. Asking the right question. How most successful people have had to work hard in order to achieve their aims. Perseverance. Resilience. Motivation. Ambition.

Rebelling against the accepted status quo. Tenacity. Self-discipline. Knowing when to move forward and when to retreat or stay where you are. Maintaining a positive self-image. Believing in your ability to reach your goals.

Willard Wigan. Recognised as the greatest Micro-artist in the world. Willard's sculptures are so small that they have to be viewed through a powerful microscope, and he is continually breaking the boundaries of what is considered possible. He talks about his struggle with severe dyslexia, and how the humiliation he experienced as a child because of this spurred him to tremendous heights of achievement.

CHAPTER 4. EVOLUTION

Life as a continually evolving process. The common denominator. Our part in this through our own ability to access our sense of purpose. How survival of any species, including the human race, is directly linked to motivation. Without the will to move forward, to progress and adapt to changes, atrophy and stagnation set in. Being open to new ideas. Seeing and acting on opportunities. Taking note of the direction current trends are moving in. Entelechy. Foresight. Trusting in and listening to the intuition. Our evolution through communication. The possibilities for the future evolution of our species.

Peter Ulrich. Musician and former percussionist for Dead Can Dance and This Mortal Coil, and the frontman for The Peter Ulrich Collaboration albums for City Canyons Records. Peter's ability to tell compelling stories and create an air of mystery through his compositions is enhanced through his openness to experimentation. He talks about how he became a musician, his connection with Dead Can Dance, and how his music has evolved and is continually evolving.

CHAPTER 5. INNOVATION

The importance of lateral as well as linear thinking. Openness to the new and untried. Experimentation. The ability to make connections between apparently diverse elements, and to incorporate them into your long-range goals. Original thinking. Exploration of the mental faculties. Insights which can be backed up through practical application. Making the connection between ourselves and the cosmos.

Dr. Sam Parnia. A graduate of Guys and St. Thomas' medical schools. Chairman of the Horizon Research Foundation, a world-wide charity that investigates the implications on the understanding of consciousness through near-death experiences. Author of *What Happens When We Die.*

CHAPTER 6. THE CREATIVE PROCESS

What is creativity? Accessing the creative principles within ourselves. The mind as the ultimate creative tool. Exploration and expression of ideas. Creating links. The effects of creativity on the physical, emotional and psychological aspects of ourselves. Manifesting ideas into reality. Tapping into the fundamental core aspect of the self in order to access patterns in the unconscious/subconscious mind, in order to work with and through them. The transformation process that takes place within and is manifested outwardly. Self-discipline. The universe as a creative entity, which is expressing its creativity through the lenses of our individual lives.

Colin Wilson. The late author of over 80 books on different aspects of the mind, the occult, biographies and investigations into the distant past. Widely recognised as one of the great thinkers of our era, he talks about how his extraordinary mind works, and how the ideas for some of his books came about.

CHAPTER 7. INSPIRATION

What is inspiration? Where does it come from? The ability to inspire yourself and others. Inspire; to fill with an urge; to breathe in. Tuning in to the deep self. The Eureka! effect. How understanding of other people can lead to increased wisdom and the sharing of knowledge. Infectious enthusiasm. 'Letting go' in order to allow new and productive energy into your life. Communication. The infectious nature of passion. Connecting with archetypal and mythological energies. The Muse. Celebrating the growth process and gaining energy through the deep emotions. Resonance.

Jean Houston. Jean Houston has inspired vast numbers of people through her many books and lecture tours. She has been called one of the greatest minds in America. The Foundation for Mind Research, founded by Jean and her husband, Robert Masters, has taken the exploration of the mind to an astonishing realisation of our capabilities. In her interview, Jean discusses the entelechy (the inner dynamic purpose), how she gains inspiration in challenging times, her relationship with the celebrated anthropologist Margaret Mead, and how myth has opened up new dimensions in her life.

CHAPTER 8. SUCCESS

What is success? How society usually evaluates success in terms of finances/prestige/fame. The reality - fulfilment; the ability to do what you enjoy and what inspires you, and to feel comfortable with and about yourself. Permission to be. How success is a state of mind. The inner and outer definitions of success, and how to work with this. A sense of adventure. Willingness to take risks. Taking pleasure in achievements. Remaining true to your personal vision. Self-expression. The equation for success.

Natalie Rogers. A pioneer of the expressive arts, and the founder of "Resume". Natalie was full professor at the California Institute of Integral Studies, the Institute of Transpersonal Psychology, and Distinguished Consulting Faculty at Saybrook Graduate School. Natalie's work has taken over that of her father, Carl Rogers, who was one of the founders of the humanistic psychology movement and the most influential psychologist in American history. In 1998, she received a Lifetime Achievement Award, "The Shining Star", for being "a pioneer in the field of integrative arts therapy, education, and consultation".

CHAPTER 9. CREATING OUR REALITY

What is reality, in an individual and collective sense? The different levels of reality – personal, subjective, collective. How our reality is perceived through, and coloured by, our emotional and mental states in the moment. A way to visualise possible realities as bubbles. Creating the life you wish for. The power of focus. Holding and embracing the vision. Determination. Following your dream. Manifestation through letting go of expectations from others. Consciously drawing your goals towards you. Using the wisdom of past experiences to show the way forward. Self-sufficiency. The ability of the mind to manifest what you focus on. Our fundamental purpose.

Joanne Harris. Bestselling author, whose book *Chocolat* was made into a film. Two subsequent books, *Blackberry Wine* and *Coastliners* are also being transferred to the big screen. Joanne talks about how she created a new reality in her life through the decision to follow her own creative impulses and portray the vision that she had in the idea for *Chocolat*.

MIND AND MOTIVATION EXERCISES

The exercises which are included at the end of each chapter in this book.

Foreword

By Paul Halpern, PhD

It is truly a joyous feeling when our minds are clear, our purposes resolute, and our footsteps hit the pavement with an unwavering stride. The sun is out and the wind seems at our back, propelling us ever forward. Nothing can go wrong, it seems.

Inevitably, though, obstacles arise, either externally or internally. Dark thunderclouds might cast a shadow on what had seemed like a perfect afternoon. Stepping into a gloppy puddle and coating one's boots with mud might make continuing on a casual walk much less inviting. Yet, even on an otherwise pleasant day, the nebulous doubts and murky fears that arise in one's mind might pose the greatest challenge of all. After all, one can raise an umbrella to the rain and watch out for wet hazards while taking a stroll, but one ultimately cannot avoid one's own mental landscape.

Momentary challenges and negative thoughts naturally arise for everyone. It is part of life. And, unfairly, some face greater or more frequent hurdles than others.

Moreover, levels of resilience seem to vary from person to person as well. It is horrific when an especially sensitive person faces a barrage of obstacles. Others may try to help out, but ultimately each and every one of us must accumulate the armour to defend one's peace of mind against one's own inner battles.

Yet luckily, as this important book shows in numerous lessons and examples, many effective strategies for regrouping after setbacks - major or minor - can successfully be learned.

Perseverance, flexibility, stamina, and optimism are all skills that might be acquired through practice. One need not be stuck in mental traps or overwhelmed by the demands of life.

In his science fiction novel, *The Mind Parasites*, Colin Wilson imagined an alien life form that thrived from the negative thinking of humans and clouded minds to prevent clarity. Surely, sometimes it does seem like unwelcome thoughts and feelings arise from malicious agents. In reality, they are naturally bound to pop up from time to time, purely because brains are complex systems that react in unpredictable ways. A certain scent, sound, or other sensation might trigger an unpleasant memory. But how we react to that feeling next might set the tone for the rest of the day. Do we simply recognize and acknowledge that undesirable thoughts or feelings regularly arise and then move on, or do we dwell on the negative and try to analyse fruitlessly what is happening - which might lead to even more unpleasant sensations?

Wilson is one of the many inspiring figures featured in this extraordinary book. Far from just a speculative writer, his literary, non-fiction works grappled with the role of society's outsiders and delved into ways to achieve optimistic clear-mindedness. His interview, along with the others in this book, including personalities from the realms of fiction, music, and other creative endeavours, is a must-read.

Mind & Motivation offers a unique collection of personal tales that are fascinating, as well as inspirational. Though timeless in its wisdom, this edition is updated for speaking to contemporary challenges. Read on, and learn from an assortment of imaginative thinkers, how to address adversity and erroneous thinking in a positive fashion. Follow the exercises and explore ways to reorient oneself toward new goals. Above all, employ the mind's creativity to learn new pathways toward personal satisfaction. It is never too late to see the world through the eyes of a child and embark on novel journeys toward unexplored kingdoms of self-realisation.

Paul Halpern PhD is Professor of Physics at the University of the Sciences, Philadelphia, and the author of 17 widely acclaimed popular science books. Paul has appeared on many television and radio shows, including the PBS series 'Future Quest,' the National Public Radio show 'Radio Times,' and 'The Simpsons.' Paul's website is http://phalpern.com/.

Introduction

How often do you wake in the morning filled with energy and sparkling with enthusiasm for the day that stretches ahead? How easy do you find it to recapture the sense of excitement and curiosity that suffused you when you were a small child? Why do some people attain success, while others founder? How can you further enhance your life? How can you find that seemingly elusive but glorious sense of fulfilment and purpose, which enables you to truly 'be yourself' and appreciate every moment?

The aim of this book is to answer those questions and to help you to reconnect with aspects of yourself that are frequently left behind in the daily processes of living. We all need to feel fulfilled and to feel useful to ourselves and to others, yet sometimes our hopes and dreams can slip into the background and we may question what life is really about. Finding what gives us a sense of purpose, and maintaining that feeling of 'rightness,' can transform every area of our lives. This quality is a thread that shines through our daily endeavours. It draws together our relationships with ourselves and with other people. It shimmers through both our work and our play, providing a core of meaningfulness and a sense of inner happiness that flows effortlessly through every moment. It inspires a sense of inner peace, and expresses itself as joy, as increased energy, as an irrepressible love affair with life.

We all experience dark moments: times of sorrow, disappointment, disillusionment, when we question what life is really all about. These are inevitable, but they should be brief reminders that we are always stronger than we think we are, and that there are ways in which we can negotiate challenging times. Those experiences, taken in context, can become fodder for the development of compassion, sympathy and empathy. This book does not make false promises of enabling a constant state of bliss, but if you work with the principles, and relate them to your own life, the shadow moments will more easily become compost that help to fertilise the seeds of new growth within you.

Although others can give guidance, we each carry the responsibility for expressing our potential, and we begin to develop that potential through a sense of purposefulness, of determining and discovering who we are and what we wish to achieve. This book is interactive. There is a pathworking meditation at the beginning of the book that can be used, if you wish, to open you up to connecting at a deep level with your fundamental sense of purpose. This can be read to you by a friend, or you can record it and listen to it. Each chapter includes exercises and questions that you can work with, and I would recommend that you use a dedicated notebook for recording your experiences. Doing the exercises entails commitment on your part, but this commitment is to yourself and no one else, and you can choose to go back and forth through the chapters and focus on the sections that most reflect what you are dealing with at that moment. Your exploration of the ideas and principles in this book is really an exploration of your deep self; it is something that you can undertake as 'me-time,' but the effects will profoundly touch others around you as well.

Your journey through this book is accompanied by others whose lives and work are an inspiration to many. The transcribed interviews at the end of each chapter offer a distillation of some of the experiences and insights of some extraordinary people whose stories can be a great encouragement in applying the principles of the book to your daily life.

Pathworking Exercise For Connecting With Your Inner Purpose

Make sure you are sitting comfortably. Now take a deep breath and breathe out fully. Now another. And another.

See yourself standing on a path. Around you are grassy banks. Trees stretch their branches towards the sky, and the sun is shining. You can feel the warmth of the sun on your skin, and a light breeze caresses your cheeks. You can smell the fresh fragrance of the clear air. Your feet are bare, and you feel strongly connected to the earth.

As you begin to walk along the path, let all of your senses play. Smell the fragrance of the flowers. Listen to the singing of the birds, the rustling of leaves in the trees, the sound of crickets chirping. Feel the air moving around you as you walk, and the sensation of the path beneath your feet. Is it made of earth, or stones, or sand? Look around you. Notice whether there are any creatures nearby. If so, are they moving towards you or away from you? Does your path follow a straight line, or does it meander? Is it clear and uncluttered, or are there rocks and boulders which you need to move around?

The path leads to a river. The water sparkles in the sunshine as if it is winking at you. At the riverside a boat is waiting for you. You step into it and it moves across the water. Does the water feel smooth, or do waves rise and fall, carrying you with them?

At the opposite shore you step out of the boat onto the riverbank. The grass feels soft and damp beneath your feet, and you feel the healing energies of earth and water flowing gently through you. Your path continues from the riverbank into a forest, and you follow it.

You come to a clearing in the trees. In the centre a fire burns within a small circle of decorated stones. You stand and gaze into the fire for a moment, and within the flames you see pictures of all that inspires you and moves you deeply. The images warm your heart, and you feel your energy increasing. You are filled with a sense of wellbeing. Stand there for a moment with that feeling, then make a wish, and leap over the fire onto your path, which leads from the other side.

The path takes you deeper into the forest. You feel safe and at home in its depths. Before you is a cave. Its entrance shimmers with crystals that send out rays of coloured light. You bend down to enter the cave, and move forward, feeling the abundant richness of the earth beneath your feet. The cave opens into a cavern lit with a warm glow, and you stand tall within it, and look around. There are objects here which remind you of the beauty and magnificence of your inner self, the self that you only share with those who are closest to you. Look at them; touch them. Take one as a reminder of your uniqueness, your specialness, and move towards the light at the end of the cave that beckons you onwards. The light guides you into a tunnel that rises upwards and leads you out of the cave.

Outside, the sunshine is radiant, and your path sparkles as you step along it. The trees have thinned out, and a grassy area opens up before you and leads to a walled temple. An intricate gate marks the entrance, and as you reach the gate you pause, aware that someone is standing behind it. The figure wears iridescent robes that shimmer in the light. You ask to be admitted, the Gatekeeper steps back, and the gate opens.

Your path takes you across a courtyard, past a fountain. Wonderful fragrances fill the air, and you hear the songs of many birds blending in harmony. At the end of the courtyard is a golden door, which opens as you approach. You step through into a spacious cool chamber filled with precious objects. Your senses respond to the colours and the beauty around you, and you feel a deep, uplifting sense of harmony and peace.

Leading off the chamber is an anteroom, lit by small lamps and candles that illuminate the rich hangings on the walls. In the centre of the room is a large cushion, and you sit down comfortably. Beside the cushion is a box with your name engraved on it. You open it to find a piece of paper inside. Written on it is a word or phrase that has significance for you, and that brings you a feeling of great joy. You read it and put the paper back into the box, knowing that you will remember the message that was given to you.

You rise and leave the room, crossing the spacious chamber, leaving through the golden door. You walk across the courtyard, retracing your steps, and leave the temple that is your inner space. You pass through the gateway, walk through the trees, re-enter the cave, and emerge from its splendid crystal entrance. You feel light, energised, and very happy. You skip through the trees, leap over the fire in the clearing, and run exuberantly through the forest towards the river. Your boat is waiting for you, and you climb in and sail to the opposite shore, noticing the sunlight sparkling off the water. At the other side, you follow the path back to the point where your journey began, and sit down comfortably on the ground.

Now you take a deep breath and breathe out. And another. And another. Now you can feel your awareness fully back in your body, back in this room. You feel relaxed but alert, and very peaceful. Wriggle your fingers and toes a little, and when you are ready, slowly open your eyes.

Chapter 1
A Sense Of Purpose

If you were to create a collage containing images of everything that symbolises pleasure and fulfilment to you, you would see a kaleidoscope of texture and colour. Within this, several pictures would stand out and give added luminosity to the others. Identifying these images gives you a clue as to what enhances a sense of purpose in your life. They are the keys to a door which opens into a new dimension: the exploration of your deep self.

We all need a purpose, a reason for being. Without it our lives would feel empty, aimless, lacking in focus, and therefore pointless. We would feel lost within a twilight world that seems devoid of meaning. The nihilist view of life as a tortuous process of pushing a heavy boulder up a steep hill, and seeing it roll back again as we struggle to the summit, is an illustration of a life without purpose: goal-less, bereft of hope; a life of despair. This is the experience of deep depression, when all feels lost, and life becomes a dark void of meaninglessness. In Chapter 6, the late great Colin Wilson, who was acclaimed as the exponent of New Existentialism, speaks of what he terms 'the spring morning feeling'; those sudden, inexplicable moments of pure joy when all feels right with the world. These moments are illuminated because suddenly, out of nowhere, everything in the fabric of our lives is imbued with meaning, and so becomes an image of the perfection of the moment. The experience of this is that of 'belonging.' It need not be a rare occurrence, as we shall discover in the following chapters.

THE SEARCH FOR MEANING

Everything that exists has purpose, and in expressing itself contributes to the complex pattern of life on an unimaginable scale. The biggest questions we can ask are "Who am I? Why am I here?" and often those questions are asked at an early age. The overriding reason for these questions is the search for meaning; for the purpose behind the myriad forms that appear to become increasingly more subtle and mysterious as they are investigated. The quest for a unified field theory, a 'theory of everything' being undertaken in quantum physics, fires the public imagination to a scale never before achieved by the sciences. This is because, for the first time, scientists are offering what could ultimately be seen as offering proof of the purposefulness of the universe. A mathematical equation could be the code to a new language: the language of the Infinite, which expresses with structured simplicity and elegance how and why the forces of creation emerged. But mystics as well as scientists are becoming increasingly excited and inspired by the possibilities inherent in this scientific search, because it hints at an underlying intelligence at a fundamental level which encompasses the entire tapestry of life. Each thread weaves into every other thread; the warp and weft of everything in existence is inextricably connected, synchronising with the delicate and complex balance of the whole. With our limited vision we are incapable of seeing the picture in its entirety, but the conclusion appears to be that life exists in order to *experience* as well as perpetuate itself.

Each cell in your body has the purpose of perpetuating life in order to contribute to the optimum functioning, health and wholeness of the living system that is your body. Similarly, we can see ourselves as cells on planet Earth, and each of the countless planetary and stellar bodies as being individual cells in the universe.

THE CLUSTERING EFFECT

All too often we feel alone, trying to fulfil our purpose without a clear awareness of what it is, and without a consciousness of being connected to the whole. But a paradigm shift in consciousness is occurring, which is drawing us to connect with like-minded others. This forms clusters of energy. The clustering effect is extremely powerful. Clusters of stars create galaxies. The clustering of cells, each with its own function, creates a body. In the evolution of life on our planet, the major changes occurred when the reproduction of cells shifted from simple cell division, where a single cell reproduced itself, to the coming together of two separate cells which then exchanged genetic information, increasing the information contained in subsequent generations. Similarly, the coming together of individuals creates groups, in which more information and knowledge can be exchanged, creating an acceleration of the evolutionary process within the human racc.

The availability of instant world-wide communication means that information, insights and knowledge can now be shared with anyone, anywhere. What were previously small, localised communities, each with their own worldview and knowledge, is now expanding, bringing about the awareness that we are all part of a global community. Our individual sense of purpose is able to more easily merge with, and be amplified by, the purpose of others. This then enhances the purpose of our planet, our solar system, our universe.

CONNECTIONS

The key to accessing this sense of purpose comes through experiencing a deeper sense of connection with the self. This leads to increased understanding of who you are, what inspires you, and which direction feels most appropriate for your growth as a person. It also leads to a more profound sense of connection with the world around us. And, like a pebble cast into a pond, the ripples from our presence in the world spread outwards far further than we realise. Every action leads to a reaction in some form, whether this is chemical and physical, or emotional, or mental.

PAYING ATTENTION TO SUBTLE MESSAGES

Intelligence is considered to be the ability to make sense of connections; to have the mental facility to recognise these, and so generate a deeper understanding of their meaning. Emotional intelligence is the key to the feelings and the imagination, to the understanding of the messages that are received symbolically and intuitively. Our emotional intelligence allows us to 'sense' solutions, to follow insights, and to relate to others. This is very apparent in many indigenous cultures where everything is viewed as symbolic, as having a personal message for the observer. This imbues each event and interaction with a deep significance that can be learned from and absorbed.

Noticing how we are affected by those around us, by the environment, the time of day and the weather, helps us to attune to our instincts and subtle emotions. Observing the creatures in the world around us becomes a reminder of qualities that can be drawn on within ourselves. An ant can teach us about the ability to work within a team for the common good. An eagle soaring high above reminds us of the need to take a higher perspective; to see the overview, the complete picture, instead of being caught up in minor details. A dragonfly hovering nearby is a message that reminds us to see through illusions which hold us back from discovering truths about ourselves, and to perceive reality in a fresh way. The dog who gives us trust and loyalty can help us to absorb those qualities and explore them in our relationships with others. Everything has a unique and specific purpose within its own group, and is also a symbolic reminder that our lives are interwoven with everything else. Wherever we choose to look, messages can be found that guide us, or open us to realisations about ourselves and life as a whole. Increasing our awareness of the events that take place around us, and our reactions to those, shows us how we shape the direction of our lives in subtle ways.

THE EXPERIENCE OF PURPOSE

Experiencing a sense of purpose indicates being aware of forward movement, of momentum, of a feeling of 'rightness.' This also helps us to see that our lives have meaning, have direction. By expressing more of the magnificence of our potential we can also reach out and touch others. Purposefulness is the energy that creates a goal, gives direction, adds impetus, generates energy, and enables us to surmount obstacles that are stepping-stones to our growth. A sense of purpose acts as a motivating factor for accomplishment, and it imbues our lives with inner meaning.

Some people are born with a distinct sense of purpose. Their lives from early on are guided by a feeling of destiny; a deep inner knowing that they have a dream which they must strive to bring to realisation. All of their focus is trained like a laser on that which will enable them to draw the vision into reality. If asked, they will often tell you that they always felt different in some way; singled-out, almost alien in their sense of otherness because their experience of being driven to single-mindedly reach their goal sets them apart from the crowd. Yet for many of us, the leading question is often "What should I be doing with my life?" and the answers are not always clear. The act of holding an attitude of openness to finding out can enable us to look at the interwoven threads in our lives, and to discover that a pattern emerges which shows us the way forward.

Life is a journey of discovery. Sometimes it can feel as if there are no clear maps or guidelines, but on inspection pathways reveal themselves which beckon us on. Sages throughout the ages have told us that the purpose of the journey is not so much the goal as the journey itself and what we learn along the way. The people we meet, the experiences we gather, the knowledge we accumulate about ourselves and the world are invaluable and are unique to us. Though we are connected to others, and touched by them, each of us experiences life subjectively. Our perceptions are coloured, shaped and moulded by the rich diversity of experiences and our *reactions and responses* to those experiences. We each view life through the lens of perception that we are looking through in this particular moment. What to one person may seem trivial and insignificant, to another will bear great importance and have life-changing consequences. In essence, we are all created from the same cosmic constituents, but we all express who and what we are through our own personal perspective. Like snowflakes, no two of us are exactly alike; and our purpose in life may correspond with, or be linked to the purpose of others, but it is still unique to us.

ALL THE WORLD'S A STAGE

Consider Shakespeare's famous words, "All the world's a stage, and all the men and women merely players." Now take this idea a little further. Imagine your life as a film. You are the leading character. You stand in the centre of the set; you speak your lines and act out your part. The scenery changes for the different acts of the production. Other actors come and go. Some are noticeably significant, others play minor roles. There are moments of drama, of love, romance, disappointment, tragedy, comedy, fear, anxiety, horror, reconciliation, denial, achievement, triumph. The film tells a story, and each scene holds a thread to the story's unfolding and can offer subtle clues as to what is to come.

How would you categorise the general atmosphere of the

film you are starring in? Is it a drama, a comedy, a romance, an adventure? Does your part in it fulfil you, or do you want to change your role, rewrite the script, bring in new characters or scenery?

If we view our lives as our own personal production, we become more empowered. Some of the film, or the characters in it, may seem superfluous or detrimental. But each of those characters are the leading actors in their own productions of life; writing their own scripts, choosing us to enter their film as well. On a larger scale, each of us inhabits a reality that exists in order for us to fulfil the purpose in life which is uniquely ours, and which we ourselves, *at a subconscious level*, are creating. That reality links in with the realities of those people whom we are influenced by. It is rather like a Venn diagram (two interlocking circles surrounded by a larger circle), with only the central connecting point being common to both us and to them.

Encircling the periphery of the Venn diagram is also the connection to something greater than our own individual minds; a force of intelligence which you could give any name to, but which could also be seen as your Higher Self, the overriding intelligence which guides our life's purpose. This is what we are accessing when events seem to fall into place to move us forward in a particular direction. The unseen reality that lies behind our personalities is like the blank screen that the film is projected onto. The mind is like the light that flashes through the images and projects them onto the screen. And the still pictures which appear to move because of the flickering light are our life-experiences.

HIDDEN PATTERNS

However, we usually shape our reality at a *subconscious* level. The subconscious mind is the layer of the psyche that is hidden from normal view and comes to the surface in the symbolic language of dreams, and which can also be accessed during deep hypnosis and meditation on symbolic systems such as mandalas. The subconscious mind is the storehouse of conditioned coded patterns that have been laid down from infancy onwards. Everything you heard and saw in your early years, every experience you had from childhood onwards, effectively hard-wired programmes into your subconscious mind because, in infancy, your mind was like a sponge, absorbing everything. There were no filters; everything was taken at face value. As we grow older it is possible to see how our re-actions are often pre-programmed responses – like those of Pavlov's famous dogs, who salivated when a bell rang because they had initially heard that sound when they were given food.

Unless you make a conscious choice to access the subconscious mind through techniques such as hypnosis, creative processes such as the arts, meditation, or other methods of investigating the origins of certain patterns, you are at the mercy of pre-conditioned responses. This limits your ability to choose the direction your life takes. Yet there are messages which can help us to perceive unhelpful patterns and liberate ourselves from them in order to discover our sense of purpose.

What we *can* see of the influence of the subconscious can be understood through a game. As a child, you may have made shadow-figures or puppets by placing your hands between a light and the wall or screen that it was illuminating. By putting your fingers into shapes, you could create rabbits, or dancing figures. In this game, observers could see the shadows created by our hands, but not our hands themselves. Similarly, we see the effects of the play of the subconscious mind, even though we cannot see the direct cause of those effects. By looking at our patterns of behaviour and responses, we can see *where* in our lives and attitudes we are behaving in a programmed, instead of spontaneous, manner. Once this is recognised, we can choose to discover *what* created those patterns. This could be something as simple as a chance comment that was made to you long ago, and which became stuck in your perception of yourself.

To return to the image of each of us as the central character in our own personal film; every person we connect strongly with throughout our lives reflects back to us the programming that we have taken on board, both negative and positive. We are each others' teachers. Yet, in adulthood, there is always a choice as to who shares a space in our lives. Sometimes it can be helpful to look at whether certain friendships or associations have a positive or negative effect on our emotions and our lives. If you constantly or consistently feel dragged down by an association, this is a sign that a liberating 'spring-clean' is necessary.

Sometimes you can strive to realise a vision of your purpose, only to find that it manifests in a very different way to your expectations of it. There is also a major difference between having *hopes* for a particular outcome, which means that you are focused on the outcome as being beneficial to you; and *expectations*, which indicates that you have a rigid idea of what the outcome will be, and are investing a great deal of emotional energy in it. Expectations indicate that you are attached to a specific view of what the outcome will be, and this can block you from being open to unforeseen possibilities or opportunities. Expectations come from a sense of wanting to grasp something. If they lead to success there is often no feeling of delight or achievement afterwards, and another goal then often appears to be more luminous. This is why we feel hurt and disappointed because matters haven't worked out as we expected them to. We block the flow, we sabotage ourselves by being rigid, by not allowing ourselves to be open to new possibilities which might be more constructive for us.

The key to understanding what you hope for versus the reality of what is manifesting in your life lies in the ability to detach yourself from your emotions around it and to look at what the experiences undergone in striving for that purpose have taught you. This can be very revealing, and ultimately it shows you how you have created that reality, even unintentionally.

SYNCHRONICITY

If you look back through your life, you will find that there were times when there was an increase in coincidences or synchronicity; when it seemed that events fell into place around you; when the right people appeared at the right time, or opportunities suddenly appeared, or flashes of insight showed you a clear way forward. Think about what you were doing at those times, and what you were aiming for. Then look at what those events or happenings led you into. Synchronicities are messages from the aspect of ourselves which Jung called the Superconscious - the intelligence that is greater than your 'small' self. They show you that you are moving in the right direction, that the path you are following is leading to something that is relevant and profound for you. If you become more aware of synchronicities, take notice of them and act on the messages they are giving you, you will find that you can subsequently act with the increased energy that is created through going with the flow. In his book *The Global Brain Awakens* Peter Russell points out that coincidences and synchronicities involving other people appear to be beneficial to both people involved in the interaction; that somehow, the needs of both are fulfilled.

At the end of this chapter you will find five exercises, including two in which you create and interpret a collage. In the collage of your life, which images shine out more brightly than the others? What helps you to feel more fulfilled? What gives you the greatest pleasure? If you carry those feelings forward into the present time, you gain energy as well as new ideas about how you can work with your sense of purpose and explore all of the many aspects of your potential more fully. What are you especially good at? What inspires you? What were you focusing on when you received a surprise opportunity, or a relevant phone call, or the person you most needed to meet at a particular time was introduced to you? Which positive qualities do people notice in you, and comment on the most? What gives you a sense of rightness, your own 'spring morning' feeling of all being well in your world? All of these are pointers to your inner purpose, which is trying to express itself, whether or not you take notice of it.

GOALS

Having a purpose implies having a goal to move towards. If you look back through your life, you will see that you had different goals at different times. Your goal as a child was to figure out how the world works, and what your place is in it, and that process is ongoing. On leaving school your goal was to either start work, take time out, or to go on to further study. Your goal in a relationship is to get to know your partner and yourself more deeply; to realise points of connection between you, and for both of you to learn about love and grow as people as a result. Underlying these are other goals, some of which you will have achieved, others which you may still be working towards, and yet others which fell by the wayside in order for you to pursue other paths.

LIVING THE DREAM

What do you dream of? What calls to you in the quiet moments when you are in a state of relaxed receptivity? If you could do anything at all, what would it be? Keep a note of your thoughts about this, because as you write them, you consolidate them in your own mind. With this may come doubts and questions. You might feel 'I can't do this - I'm not talented enough, or patient enough, or strong enough to reach for my dream and draw it into my life.' At this point, it is very helpful to write it all down, very quickly so that you don't start to intellectualise it. In your journal, draw a line down the centre of the page from top to bottom. On the left side, write down what you most want to do, or to achieve, or to be in your life. On the right-hand piece of paper, write down all of the qualities and resources you have which could aid your progress. Take another page and draw a line down the centre. On the left side of the paper, write down any obstacles that you think could block you. On the right side, write down any solutions you can see to those obstacles. You may be surprised at how clear the way forward towards your goal actually is. We often create doubts or obstacles that are actually excuses to not act, and these will be looked at in depth in Chapter 3.

EXPRESSING YOUR PURPOSE

When you are stepping out towards fulfilling your purpose, other people who are also moving forward tend to appear in your life. The saying 'like attracts like' is very apt. As your energy grows stronger, a magnetic field is created around you that, like a magnet and iron filings, draws others with a similar energy. The clustering effect becomes noticeable. Being around kindred spirits will help bounce the energy in all of you even higher, and it will point the way to fresh possibilities that can be beneficial for everyone.

Behind our personal sense of purpose resides a higher purpose which is not touched by our emotional, mental or material states. This higher purpose is the true reason for your goals and your motivation. It is created by the desire of your essential self, or your higher self, to express your inner beauty, harmony and unity as fully as possible, and to fully realise your connectedness with the life-force. So, what is this mysterious and numinous higher self? It is your essence, within which is contained the potential and the propensity for the most profound expression and manifestation of who and what you truly are.

Energy is never destroyed. It only changes from one form

to another. Even the energy of a great star which has collapsed upon itself to create a black hole, one of the most intriguing cosmological studies, still exists as some form of energy. We contain within the fabric of every cell in our bodies some heavy elements which are beyond iron, and which could only have been created by a supernova which exploded billions of years before the birth of our sun. The question of what intelligence created the universe is essentially the same as the question of what created us, and all other life. The fundamental truth common to both science and mysticism is that there is a pattern and a purpose within creation, and within all of its diverse forms. If an intelligence (whether we choose to perceive that as a deity or a scientific principle) underpins the existence of atoms, quarks and stars, we would be very arrogant to believe that it is not also the driving force behind our own lives.

A HIGHER VIEW

The Superconscious is an intelligence which transcends human or everyday consciousness. It is the grand overview, the unification of all aspects of yourself, and is accessed through deep meditation, flashes of intuition and inspiration; moments of absolute *knowing* which are indescribably powerful because they are inexplicable and irrevocable. The momentary experiences of the Superconscious enable a state of indisputable recognition of unity to be experienced and recognised by the conscious mind. What underlies this energy is pure consciousness. It is like the ocean that contains each drop of water. These flashes of insight contain within them a taste and fragrance of an intelligence that is greater than our small, egocentric selves. It becomes increasingly accessible when we are prepared to discard our limiting self-perceptions and realise that the song of life contains countless chords, and each of us adds our own note to the harmony.

The path through life is the journey to the recognition of

our interconnectedness with all that exists. The steps we take on that path are created through the choreography of our higher purpose, and are designed to lead us to a clearer, more profound relationship with our potential and our true nature. This is accessed through the lessons we learn along the way, and what we do with those; how we express them, the choices we make; the growth processes that we rise through in order to truly experience who we are and why we are here.

Reminder: You are expressing elements of yourself in every moment of your life.

Question to consider: In this moment, what gives you the strongest feeling of fulfilment?

EXERCISES

Exercise 1. Feeling good

In your journal, write a list of anything that makes you feel good. You can score the items on your list between 1 (for nice) and 5 (for wonderful). At the end of each day when you write in your journal, see how many feel-good points you have scored.

Exercise 2. Collage

You will need: Some magazines, scissors, glue, an A4 piece of card or paper, (optional) decorative glitter, ribbon

- Ensure that you will not be disturbed.
- Leaf through the magazines and cut out any pictures or words that have significance for you.
- Without using the glue, arrange your chosen images and words on the A4 paper. Shuffle them

around until they feel 'right.'

- Glue them down and add decorations or embellishments if you wish.
- Once you have finished, sit back and look at your collage. Observe whether there are spaces that look 'full' or have gaps. What do you feel about the images you have chosen?

Exercise 3. Interpreting your collage

- Divide your collage into halves.
- The upper half shows what you are conscious of, and your hopes and plans for the future.
- The central line reveals where your focus lies at this moment.
- The lower half reveals messages from your subconscious mind. This can provide clues to inner, hidden motivations, and can also reveal influences from the past that you may not have considered.

Exercise 4. Coincidences and synchronicities

Note down any coincidences or synchronicities in your journal. How did you feel when these occurred? What was happening at the time when you noticed the synchronicities? What did these lead into?

Exercise 5. Pinpointing your goal

In your journal, write down what you most wish for in your life. Then list any gifts or skills that you can use or develop. Do you view your goal as accessible?

PETER RUSSELL

INTRODUCTION TO PETER RUSSELL

Peter Russell's work has contributed greatly to the building of bridges between the sciences and spirituality, and encourages the emerging vision of ourselves as co-creators of not only our own destiny, but also the future of our planet. He gained an honours degree in physics and experimental psychology, and a masters degree in computer science at the University of Cambridge, England, and studied under Stephen Hawking. His interest in consciousness and Eastern philosophy led him to India, and his research into the nature of the mind, coupled with his scientific approach, has helped to facilitate a deeper awareness of ourselves and our purpose, and the vision of the universe itself as an evolving, conscious being.

Peter was instrumental in bringing personal development programmes to business, and his ground-breaking books on human and global evolution and the nature of consciousness have inspired readers and thinkers around the world. His books have been translated into 15 languages, and include 'The TM Technique', 'The Brain Book', 'The Upanishads', 'The Global Brain Awakens', 'The Creative Manager', 'Waking Up In Time', 'The Consciousness Revolution' and 'From Science To God'. He has also made 2 award-winning vidcos, 'The Global Brain' and 'The White Hole in Time'. He lectures widely, incorporating his scientific understanding with a profound vision of the possibilities that are open to us.

Pete's website www.peterussell.com is a treasure trove of information.

PETER RUSSELL

People sometimes ask me "What was the event that changed your life, and made you interested in bringing together the sciences and metaphysics?" I think both worlds were always there. I was always interested in science – I knew I was going to be a scientist when I was 6 or 7 years old. It was part of my life. And looking back, I can see the interest in the mind and consciousness was also there as a thread. In my teenage years I was playing around with hypnosis, and building machines to force my alpha waves into patterns, and reading books about out of body experiences. I think it was inevitable that the two should gradually come together. And I suppose my scientific training has led me to develop a certain way of looking at the world, and I applied that to looking at spiritual issues. I don't see any conflict between science and spirituality. I think there's conflict between the current worldview of scientists and the worldviews of many spiritual traditions. But I think you can be totally scientific about being spiritual, in terms of the approach, which is basically seeing what works, being open-minded, checking with other people to see what they find works, and progressing to a path which is narrowing down to finding out what the truth is. That's as valuable in terms of the metaphysics or consciousness stuff as it is to do with the physical world.

It came together for me when I was at university. That's when I got much more seriously interested in consciousness, to begin with. That's when I decided to move away from physics and start studying psychology, as a way of beginning to understand the brain and consciousness. There have been many little things along the way which have increased my understanding or interest, but it's been a gradual evolution; fine-tuning it as I've gone on through life.

There are several aspects to the main focus of my life. I think the primary focus is understanding the nature of the human mind. Seeing this as really being the great unexplored frontier. We know so much about the physical, material world. We know nothing really about consciousness – how we get ourselves trapped, how we live with ourselves. And a lot of the religious traditions, particularly those in the East, have really explored that. They're really psychologies that were framed in pre-scientific eras. And I think the psychology there is very profound. So my basic thrust is re-discovering what that core message is, translating it into terms which are appropriate to this time, this culture. Working with it in myself is primary, because it's no good just preaching stuff if you're not doing it. But also, I'm the only person I have real responsibility for in this world. And just like everyone else, I've got enough stuff to work on in myself, to free myself, and that's a big enough challenge. The rewards of that are wonderful – just to clean up my own life feels so much better; whenever I do things or make breakthroughs, that's wonderful. And that is the basis on which I can then have more to give to other people, from my own experience of what works, what doesn't work, the journeys I've been through.

So, I see the primary focus as exploring, almost distilling, the perennial wisdom in my own life down to what I see as key things, and then disseminating that out to others.

The secondary thrust is a whole historical perspective on these times, because I've always been interested in where we are in history – and not just in human history, but in evolutionary history. And that means both looking back at the past, and evolutionary trends, and what's brought us to this point, and seeing why this point in our evolution is so significant. But this also means moving into the future – moving along the timeline the other way. I use that to contextualise the inner work, because I see more and more that the real challenge that we're up against at this time is a spiritual crisis – a crisis of consciousness. How the coming years unfold is going to be very much a reflection of our consciousness, our values, our perception. If we by and large remain stuck in self-centred, very limited modes of consciousness, materialistic thinking, I don't think we have much chance of making it through. So I think the real challenge is…can we really discover now, in this time, what it is that the great teachers have been telling us for thousands of years, and which has always been useful for individuals, but now is becoming a collective imperative. Can we actually begin to do that? To wake up to who we are, what it really means to be a conscious being, and discover that wisdom that can free us. Because I think what we really need today is that inner freedom. We have incredible external freedoms, but very little inner freedom. And it's because of our lack of freedom on the inside that we're abusing and misusing our external freedoms.

So, my main focus is really the exploration of the inner, and contextualising it. I think, particularly in this area, there's nothing new under the sun. The wisdom is ageless wisdom that people can pick up and read in books almost anywhere. There are numerous books to read, and numerous traditions. But also, I think it's a wisdom that we all carry inside us. We *know* these truths anyway, deep down inside us. But it's almost as if our culture is in conspiracy against us knowing this – they want us to keep focused on the material things; on doing and buying and fitting in and being 'good', externally oriented people. And yet deep inside we know it's a sham, and that basic wisdom is there in each of us. It's so covered over by all the belief systems, assumptions, the ideologies that are fed to us through our culture, that we don't really acknowledge it. And I think one of the most important things to do today is to remind each other of that basic wisdom. The value of spiritual texts is not that they *teach* us something, but that they remind us of what we already know, deep inside, so that we can actually bring it more into light, more into consciousness within ourselves.

To come back to the self-awareness. It's like we're *half-awake* at the moment. Self-awareness is a gradually emerging thing. You can look at other animals, look at our cousins the great apes. There's a little self-awareness there. A chimpanzee, if you put a spot on its forehead and show it a mirror, will realise it's looking at itself, and will try to scratch the spot off. So, it has a biological self-awareness. This doesn't work with a cat. If you put a cat in front of a mirror, it doesn't think there's another cat there. It knows there's something weird going on. It doesn't seem to recognise itself, but it knows it's not actually another cat. It's probably totally puzzled, and it's too much for it to accept.

Self-awareness is a gradually evolving thing. With human beings, what has really given us a greater self-awareness is language. Because with language, through the internalised language of being able to think, to reflect upon our experiences, we become aware that we are aware, on a cognitive level. And also, anthropologists see how in very simple societies there is much less sense of individuality. Our cultures accentuate that individuality. So, I think our self-awareness has been an awakening thing. It's not something that suddenly happens; it's an evolving process of becoming more and more self-aware.

We're caught at a point where we have very strong individual self-awareness, and obviously we think that's the end of the journey. But what all the great mystical teachings have said is – beyond that, or behind that individual awareness is a much richer, much deeper sense of identity, which is an awareness that what we call the Self is just consciousness itself. What we call the "I" is in a sense an illusion we get caught in; it seems very, very real. When you actually explore what we mean by "I", and really look at that, what you really mean is just that fundamental basis of all existence. To me, the "I" is a *feeling* of *being.* It's the feeling of consciousness. But because we don't know that, and we get caught in a sense of individuality, we try and clothe this sense of "I"ness in various things, to give us a sense of feeling a unique being. And so we clothe it in terms of our characteristics, our personalities, how other people see us, what we do, what we think, our history, our family. All of this goes towards creating this sense of "I". We then feel very happy and secure because now we know who "I" am. But of course that isn't who we are at all. These are things we have chosen to identify ourselves with. But if we get stuck in that mode, that sense of identity is very vulnerable and fragile. Because if the things we identify with change, or if someone criticises us, or whatever, if we lose the things we hold on to, then we have to reassert or reaffirm our sense of identity. I think a lot of what goes wrong in the world really comes from that – from people's need to continually bolster their sense of who they are. Their sense of identity, from relationship issues to political issues, corporate issues; a lot of it comes back to the need to continually affirm our sense of self, or defend it in some way – to be seen as a certain sort of person.

So, I think that as we increase or expand our awareness to see a deeper level of being behind this individual, illusory sense of self - to see what's behind it - then we free ourselves from that need to continually reaffirm that sense of self, which is why Indian teachings talk about a "sclf-libcration". Thc frccing of the self, the liberation of the self.

And when we are living in this self-liberation, much of that stuff is seen as no longer important. We are self-sufficient. We just know this feeling – that this is me, and I can't define it, but that's fine and it's great, and I feel centred in it.

The other thing that happens is that in our culture we've got caught in a belief system which I think most cultures get caught up in. But it's particularly strong in our culture, that whether or not we are happy or at peace depends upon what we have in the world, what we do, how others see us. So we get caught in what I call the materialistic mind-set, which says in order to be happy you have to have and do the right things. And what all the great teachings have said is that as your awareness increases, you realise that's not true at all. It's about *how* you see things – whether or not you're at peace is a reflection of how you look at the world. And as our awareness expands, we become free again from that mode of thinking. So that rather than thinking 'if only I had more of this, or this thing', we'd be happy; we would realise that we're at peace anyway. When we discover those deeper levels of consciousness, they are peaceful states. We don't *need* to look out there, and continually take from our surroundings or from other people in order to be at peace.

And the third thing is that all traditions say that when you get in touch with that deeper level of being, it's also a state of love – not in a romantic sense; it's a deep sense of unconditional love. And that again is something that's sorely missing in our culture – it's a reflection of what's called the egocentric mode of consciousness, which is almost the opposite to love.

So in terms of where we're going, I think if we can begin to explore our consciousness, and discover these levels behind the everyday mode of functioning, we'll become more free of most of the impediments that really screw up our culture. So in terms of where it could go, at one level it could be a world in which we wouldn't be governed by fear, by egocentricity, by anxieties about what might or might not happen to us. It would be a culture in which we would be coming much more into a state of knowing our inner security, and it would be a much more compassionate world. And at the same time, technology is taking us into a world that is increasingly globalised. We're seeing that already. I think we're going to need those sorts of shifts in order to actually begin to function as a global community. Otherwise we're still going to be full of antagonism, or feeling separate from each other; we need that deeper sense of oneness to begin to function together collectively.

Our search for meaning is certainly fuelling the scientific search, but it's more as a search for understanding of the cosmos. And what that's done in recent times is show that you can't just look at the physical world, and not look at the inner world. What we're seeing in modern physics is that the observer is somehow involved with the physical world in ways that no-one quite understands or knows how to interpret. We just know something weird is going on. And I think what has occurred in the path up to the beginning of this century is that we thought we could ignore the mind; that the physical world was out there, on its own. That really goes back to Descartes, who decided, in order not to get burnt at the stake or imprisoned by the Vatican, to say "We empiricists will study the physical world, and we'll leave the world of the mind and spirit to the church – we won't tread on your ground". That was the history of science for a couple of hundred years, then with quantum theory and relativity we started realising that it isn't quite like that; you can't separate the two.

Again, it comes back to inner knowing. That there is this inner knowing, that it is all one, that we are all connected; and how we are inside does affect the external world, and there is much more potential to human consciousness than we normally think. We are not just machines operating as a result of what goes on in the brain. We have this intuition, and so when science starts finding things that tell us, "Hang on, consciousness *is,* it *cannot* be totally ignored; it is involved in some way", it resonates with that intuition, and we realise this is important, it's getting closer to the truth, it becomes more interesting.

For a single breakthrough, it's probably the one of the greatest shifts in scientific thinking. To realise that it's not just a physical machine out there, but that actually our inner world is intimately involved in what goes on out there. That's why I think all the stuff on non-locality in physics is getting so exciting for people. Things don't operate quite as mechanically as we thought; there's mystery out there. I do think that what's really going on is probably beyond human comprehension – we get this arrogance at times that because we can do so much with our minds, we can fully understand the cosmos. Here we are, this ape that has language and a bit of technology, *(laughs)* who says what consciousness is capable of – this is just our current stage. And human beings may be incapable of ever comprehending what's actually happening at the quantum level.

In terms of purpose, this goes back to where we started. I got interested in the Gaia theory through reading Teilhard de Chardin in the late '60's. I came across some magazines from "The Teilhard Review" a couple of days ago. Looking through them, in 1967 there was somebody writing about "What are we doing to the Earth's atmosphere? Are we upsetting the oxygen/carbon dioxide balance? And will we start disrupting the weather system to our detriment?" This was in 1967. But Teilhard de Chardin saw evolution as a spiritual journey, and saw the collective awakening of humanity as the end point of evolution; of humanity en masse achieving the sorts of realisations and states of consciousness that before had been only attained by the odd saint, sage or guru. He saw that we're moving towards everybody having that sort of awakening.

That resonated with something deep inside me, and then when the Gaia hypothesis came along, I immediately gravitated towards that. Because that, again, was talking about the Earth as being a single living being. Then it struck me – what is humanity doing on the planet? What is our role? Because in terms of evolutionary time, we're just the last 1% of 1% of the history of life on Earth. We're one thousandth of the history of life on Earth. Suddenly this species has appeared, and the planet has done very well without us, whereas the rainforests have been here for billions of years, evolving and changing. And the planetary system, Gaia, has been operating very well. Now, in the last one thousandth of its history, this young upstart has appeared. What are *we* doing? We're not actually necessary at all for the planet. If humanity disappeared, the planet would get on very well (probably a lot better) without us.

Then I realised that what *we* do (like the rainforests exchange carbon dioxide for oxygen) is process information. That's what human beings are good at. Which led me to the idea that maybe we're becoming like the brain of the planet. And I suddenly realised there were a lot of parallels between the way a human brain grows in the foetus, and the way we're wiring ourselves up and connecting ourselves together. And so I was seeing that there was this synergy of where information technology was taking us, and where our spiritual awakening was taking us was all moving towards this collective global awakening. And the thing that gives me most hope that this is happening is actually seeing what is happening from one generation to another. It's not so much what is happening in individuals.

What we're talking about is a profound shift in worldview; the most profound paradigm shift that has ever happened in human beings. Because it's not just about a paradigm shift in physics, or biology; we're talking about a profound shift in worldview that's traditionally called enlightenment, or awakening, liberation. When an individual has that, it's a whole different way of experiencing your life. We're talking about this on a collective level.

Now, when you look at paradigm shifts in science, they generally don't happen because individual scientists wake up and change their minds. They tend to hold on to their old way of seeing things, then a new generation comes up, adopting a new way of looking at things. That's what I see is happening today. What I call the kids (they'd probably be insulted to be called that, but teenagers, people in their early 20's) have *so* much wisdom, understanding and compassion. That simply was not there when I was that age. I'm not saying they're all like it, but even if it's just ten or twenty percent, a lot of them are. When I was that age, back in the 60's, we thought we were pretty hip, and for the standards of that time we probably were. But we'd be totally naïve now.

If you could take one of these kids, put them in a time machine, and send them back to the 60's, people wouldn't know what to make of them. Apart from the fact that they have tattoos, and body piercings, and ride skateboards, with their understanding and the wisdom they have about life they would have been seen as super-gurus or something. And we don't realise how much our culture has changed. That has happened because of a lot of different things. I think a large part of it is parenting, the way we bring up our children in a more humane, compassionate way. The growing awareness of parents rubs off on children and how they look at life. The amount of information that's available – in the media, on the internet – particularly around environmental and political issues, is much greater.

So, the combination of all those things, and probably many others, means that a child growing up today is standing basically on the shoulders of its parents. So whatever state of consciousness or awareness the parents have reached is where the children are starting off. I think it was Buckminster Fuller who said that if you want to know who your elders are, look to your children. We think about the wise people as being only those who have lived 70 years on the planet, and sussed out what it's all about. But equally true, there are kids of 16 who have also sussed out what it's all about – they are as wise as the elders. This wisdom is leaping generation by generation. I see people in their 20's doing incredible work with incredible enthusiasm, and they're having children. What are *those* children going to be like, as they grow up standing on the shoulders of what we now see as great lights of wisdom? Who knows? In another 20 years, we'll have beings who, if you could put them in a time machine and bring them back to *now,* would seem absolutely phenomenal and beyond our comprehension.

So that's what gives me the greatest hope – the generational shifts that are happening. And that's where you would expect them. We're doing our work, and getting better and freer, and we're preparing the way for the next generation to stand on our shoulders and leap ahead, and then people will stand on *their* shoulders and leap ahead.

In accomplishing that inner awakening, I think we have the knowledge – most of the knowledge – we need. So it's not about gaining new knowledge in how to accomplish it. I think the first thing is the motivation to actually want to do it, because it does take a willingness to make that the focus of your attention. Some of it you can do as you go through life, but it's about seeing life in the context of inner learning; of learning where you get yourself trapped, and how to free yourself up. And the motivation comes from realising that life becomes much better, more fun, more enjoyable. The more free you become inside, the better it is, and so it is actually worth having the focus and making that deliberate choice. So, one needs to be willing to make these explorations. Also, something I touched on earlier, which is being scientific about it, which means being willing to be open-minded, to explore various things, to see what works. So that if something's not working, you can discard it – you don't have to do it because some guru says it's the way to go. You have to decide for yourself what seems to work for you, what seems to free you – to bring you joy.

There's also the potential today which hasn't been there before, for synergy between different things that help you in awakening. If you were living a couple of hundred years ago, in India, the only way you would have had was with your teacher, who would probably have told you a certain practice of meditation, and that might have taken you a certain way. Now you could combine that with some form of therapy that might give you a greater understanding of how you're blocking yourself. Or with some form of self-hypnosis, or autosuggestion, or biofeedback, or being aware that diet is important; that your mind is a reflection of what you put into your body. There could be many different things which together could actually enhance each other. That's an area we haven't fully explored in our culture. I think there's room to experiment and find out how practises can enhance each other, and take you further, faster.

Recognising that we are a learning community is helping.

And supporting each other on the path. Being reminders to each other of what we're actually here for, what our lives are about, what we really want them to become. Because we so easily get sucked into the materialist mind-set of the culture, of gaining satisfaction through achieving external goals, which deep down we know isn't true. We need those continual reminders from each other that it's just a blind alley. If you just turn on the television or pick up a newspaper you can be sucked straight back into it. So how do we find the strength to stand up for what we know inside? I think that the more we can remind each other, the more we can validate the internal path, and inspire each other to be on that journey.

And also (and this is a personal thing of mine) stripping away the spiritual language. I think so many of the teachings are being handed down to us in terms of the language and culture of the times they were discovered, which were great then, but don't have a lot of meaning for us today. The basic process in which the mind gets trapped, the basic principles behind freeing the mind haven't changed. They just need to be put in language that is appropriate to our time and culture. And that, to me, is really the language of psychology; an understanding of what happens with us. So as we do that, we make it much more respectable and understandable, which validates it enough for us to take it seriously and do more research on it. So I think it's not really about discovering anything new, but it's about facilitating what's already happening – what is there. A cross-fertilisation of each other, and processes and techniques.

I find inspiration through spiritual teachings in the form of spiritual texts, because that's the main way we have access to what's been handed down. People find it strange when I say this, but although I'm a writer, I read very, very little these days. My writing comes out from inside me, and for 10 years now I haven't done much of sitting in libraries and reading books. When I read, it's generally books which I find inspiring, which touch into that inner knowing – so they're usually good, great spiritual texts of one form or another. And I like to start off every day with some form of reading, just to remind me of those deeper intuitions; to carry them with me into the day.

People who are 'living it' are a great inspiration. Just seeing people who have, in their own way, found a lot of inner freedom and compassion. I find it very inspiring just to see their lives, to be around them.

I'll tell you that also my Self, in a strange way, inspires me. But not the superficial, individual sense of self. Just when I'm in a clearer, cleaner state of mind, experiencing being in touch with that deeper, more universal level of consciousness. Just tasting that makes me want to say "Yes! This is what I want. This is what I want more in my life".

And what I find funny is that the memory of those states sticks more strongly than any other memory. Normally memory works by association, connections, and here are states of consciousness which are so divorced from everyday reality, yet the memory of them is so palpable. Just knowing those states which are so self-inspiring makes you want more of them.

Chapter 2
Motivation

Motivation is the driving force that keeps us alive. In its most primitive aspect it takes the form of a survival instinct. Motivation is the underlying reason why we wake each morning. It is what keeps our hearts beating and our lungs transferring oxygen around our bodies. It is the hidden reason behind our yearnings, our wishes, and our dreams. It is the supreme embodiment of the life-force within us longing to be expressed through every moment that we inhabit our bodies. Without motivation we fade away, we lose the will to carry on, we become shadows who forget our connection with who and what we are, and what we can become.

At the beginning of our lives, it is this force that causes us to cry out, to draw the first stinging breath of air into our lungs, to yell when we are hungry, afraid, lonely, or in pain. At this stage motivation is instinctive, a primal urge which ensures our survival. Our parents have been programmed by Nature to hear, to listen, to intuit, and to respond to our needs. Their motivation is our survival as well as their own.

As babies, it was motivation that kept us curious, that made us look at our surroundings and try to make sense of them, that drove us to grasp the hand offered to us, to strive to work out the complex dynamics of crawling, walking, feeding ourselves, speaking in a language that those around us could understand. This curiosity, the innate need to know, helped us to feel more in control of ourselves and our environment, and opened up new landscapes within us as well as externally, creating more subtle connections within the brain as we moved from crawling to walking. Through our interaction with the world around us, we came to perceive ourselves - initially as part of the whole, then as separate beings. In later years, that searching and yearning becomes channelled into finding a way back to that space within us which denies a sense of separation; that longs for unity with ourselves, with other human beings, and with whatever name you choose to give to the Ultimate.

It is motivation that helps us to spell out our hopes, our needs, and our goals. It is what enables us to overcome obstacles, to rejoice in triumphs and achievements, and to take action to preserve ourselves when the risks presented seem too great. A motive is a *reason,* conscious or unconscious; it spurs us on, moves us forwards, and gives purpose to all that we think, feel, and do.

THE SYMPHONY OF LIFE

Every form of life, from a sub-atomic particle to a plant, animal, human being, planet and star, is guided by physical laws that hold the tenacious threads of matter in place. The universe is like an instrument, wherein the music creates form. In some native cultures, myths describe how the world and all its creatures were sung into being. Everything in existence has its own particular vibration; each of us holds our own particular vibratory resonance, like a musical note. And the combined notes blend together to create a symphony – the music of the cosmos.

The underlying purpose of this symphony enables the perpetuation of life; the continuation of a harmonic dance that encompasses each and every form of life within its intricate and delicate choreography. The life-force within us demands to be expressed purely because it exists, and as individuals we each have our own purpose for being here. We are adding our notes to the song and our steps to the dance in order to learn, to grow, to evolve, to fulfil our potential, to connect with the creative source of our being, and to contribute to the beauty and harmony of the whole.

THE POWER OF DESIRE

A primary quality that motivation engenders is desire. This creates focus, generates energy, gives impulse to creativity and conjures form out of formlessness. Desire drives conscious intent. When you desire something – a relationship, a material belonging, knowledge, or union with the Ultimate, the singular mode of consciousness immediately becomes aware of a state of duality. There is suddenly an observer and an object, perceiver and perceived. Things are seen in terms of opposites; there is an awareness of the presence or the absence of what is desired. A sense of separation occurs. A focus on the absence of the desired objective creates a sense of loss; the presence of that which is longed for creates a feeling of security and fulfilment. The insights gained through modern physics have proven that through the simple act of observation the observer changes the behaviour of the observed. Nothing is static. Our desires create a ripple of action and reaction, viewed by us as having positive or negative results. And whether the focus of our desire is drawn towards us or shifted away from us depends upon our attitude towards it.

The question that we need to ask ourselves frequently is whether our attitude is fear-based or love-based. Motivation that rests in fear is what gives rise to the selfish impulses, grasping and greed that have led to much personal and collective misery and the current ecological crisis. It is the fear of lack; that we will not have enough for our survival. Desire for the gratification of immediate wants or needs, with no thought or consideration for long-term consequences, has repercussions that can ring out far into the future. This keeps us 'small,' contracts the free expression of our energy, creates negative and selfish thinking patterns, and fosters increasingly more insecurity.

The love-based motivational impulse of desire urges us to access a deeper sense of harmony and fulfilment within ourselves and fosters our awareness of unity with others. Through working with, and generating that, in our environment, a greater sense of personal, domestic, political, ecological and global harmony is generated. We can then truly fulfil our sense of purpose. So how can we act consciously to direct the course of our lives to harmonise with our own inner purpose? How can we join the dance of life with more awareness of our particular gifts, an increased understanding of what we truly want, and the power to create this? How can we acknowledge and nurture what we are capable of blossoming into? And with that realisation, how can we move forward surely and confidently, knowing that the state of fulfilment that we seek is there within us, waiting to be experienced and expressed?

BECOMING CLEAR

The first step is to know what you want. This sounds simple, but many people move through life with no clear idea of what they really want. We wonder what life is really about, what we're doing here on this beautiful life-filled globe that floats through space. It is important to find out what, in an individual sense, helps you to express more of who you are. What fills you with a feeling of passion for life? What fires you up, sends a ripple of recognition through you? The possibilities are endless, but the crux of all the options available to you is the discovery of a sense of wholeness and connectedness within you. Only you know what creates a spark within you that makes you want to shout an almighty "Yes!" to life.

So, sit down now and think about it. What motivates you? Write it down. Use your imagination to create on a sheet of paper the image of the life you wish for. Explore your wildest dreams and fantasies. Add to it whenever something new occurs to you. Consider what lights a spark of inspiration within you. Open yourself to the knowledge that you can create and re-create your life purely by focusing on your goals and working to draw them into your life. Set it in the present time, as the future is created from the energy that you are working with now, the thoughts that you focus on, the reality that you perceive yourself to be in at this very moment.

Now look at your list, often. Hone it down so that it starts to become a plan, a map, a landscape that you can begin to explore and follow, and that directs you onwards towards your goals. Keep in mind that there are no horizons. You are a being of infinite potential that you are now in the process of realising. And look at what can be, and needs to be, done in order to help you to fulfil your goals.

Usually, the wilder your dreams are, the more effort you need to put into accomplishing them. But often, because you are focused, the universe will show that you are moving in the right direction by offering a helping hand in the form of a stroke of luck, synchronicities, or opportunities along the way. There is a distinction between effort, which entails putting energy into what you are aiming for, and struggle, which involves feeling bogged down and discouraged by it. Keep an eye on the terrain: are you prepared to accept and work with the bumpy areas? Are you willing to hang on in there when things seem to be moving slowly? It is necessary to think seriously about what you want, and to decide whether you are willing to accept the responsibility that goes with it. You may find, when you have looked at your list a few times, that what you truly want varies from what you initially thought you wanted. If so, make the adjustments.

Every person alive desires recognition for something; it further affirms our sense of self. And we all deserve it, even if it just takes the form of an acknowledgement with a smile from someone dear to us. But the most important person who can give you the recognition you merit is *yourself*. When it comes down to basics, if *you* don't feel good about your life, the opinions of others won't count for anything in your own eyes. And others will take you at face value, and constantly mirror back the messages that you are putting out to them.

SELF-BELIEF

The first step is to begin to believe in yourself. Remind yourself over and over that you can achieve your goals. Start to really take notice of the qualities within you that make you unique. See yourself as beautiful, empowered, positive, and raring to go. Tell yourself you are a person who is now ready to direct the course of your life. Once you make that decision within yourself, the wheels are set in motion and things start to happen which affirm this to you. When you are aiming for your goals, also be aware that the external manifestation only brings satisfaction if you are attuned to your inner needs, those which lead to a sense of finding peace and harmony within yourself.

What makes one person more motivated than another is a combination of determination and belief in the ability to create change. If you believe that you are capable, and worthy, then you are able to express this outwardly. If you believe that the world is out there, just waiting for you, then you will find that it is so. It's all a matter of confidence, and the more you tune into what is going well in your life, the more your confidence will grow.

Most people are conditioned from childhood that they are small and powerless; that the world out there is big and hungry and will eat them up for breakfast; that everyone else is bigger and better than them; that if they believe in themselves, others will try and knock them down. The truth is that you are a vast, infinite being, awash with gifts, talents, and potential, arriving on this planet with a yearning to discover just who and what you truly are.

Make a decision right now to believe in yourself and what you are doing, and be prepared to stand alone if you need to. 'Alone' also means 'all one,' a state of being in which you are able to experience a sense of completeness within yourself. You are in the process of nurturing your dreams, bringing them from one possible future, out of many hypothetical ones, into a concrete part of your life. You are preparing to birth yourself. This involves the conception of your dreams, the fertilisation, the germination process, the nourishing of what aids you, the transition between the old, limited you and the new, empowered you, and the birthing - the moment when you see the physical and material fruits of your efforts.

THE QUALITIES OF MOTIVATION

There are qualities that you can call upon to help you along the way. These are love and acceptance of self, determination to succeed, focus, self-discipline, energy, enthusiasm, rebellion, and confidence.

Loving and accepting yourself is a challenge for most of us. This is the ability to get to know yourself. It means understanding your motives and viewing what you see as your positive and negative qualities with an air of detachment. This helps you strive to develop the positive traits and to work constructively with the negative ones. It involves accepting yourself as a person who is learning, and growing, and loving the essence of who you are. It means accepting that mistakes are made and can be learned from. And it is ultimately the realisation that you have a right to be here, that your life has meaning, and that there is an inner beauty within you that can be allowed to shine through everything you do.

Determination is the ability to keep going, to hold your goals in sight, to refuse to allow other factors to distract you from what you set out to achieve. Determination means that if someone says that what you are aiming for is impossible, you can calmly disagree and go your own way without feeling discouraged. Determination enables you to overcome obstacles by seeing them as challenges that just make you stronger. Determination helps you stick with long-range goals and to keep your sights set on them when the going seems tough. Determination is holding the dream in your heart and staying with it. The degree of your determination is the barometer that you can use to feel whether this is what you really want in your life.

Focus is intense concentration. It is the ability to employ tunnel-vision, to see your goal as already accomplished, to *feel* it as real within yourself, and to allow it the space to manifest itself. Focus also involves being aware of other factors around you that can be drawn in to help; it is like a magnet that you can activate within you. Another term for focus is one-pointedness. Be single-minded in your approach and be open to the emergence of new possibilities and opportunities that will make themselves clear when you see your goal as a target. See your will as the arrow that is aimed surely at its mark.

Self-discipline is the art of knowing what is helpful to you and what hinders you, and of sticking with what you need to do to achieve your goal. If you wish to be a long-distance runner, you need to train for it. If you want to be a great artist, or musician, or writer, or actor, or doctor, or technician, you have to immerse yourself in your craft, study, practice, learn from others, and be willing to make mistakes along the way that will teach you even more. If you yearn to connect more deeply with the spiritual aspect of yourself, you need to meditate and keep a check on whether you are living your life in a manner that helps you to evolve. Self-discipline is the ability to wake up each morning with your action plan in your head, and to go out there and put it into operation. It is also about setting yourself limits that are reasonable for you, and ensuring that you give yourself time to sleep, eat, and have some fun, without allowing yourself to make excuses for not getting on with the work you have set yourself to do. It's about realising what your avoidance tactics are and refusing to play their game. If you find yourself procrastinating, make a firm decision to make no more excuses, and to put your plans into action. It's the nitty-gritty of getting on with the task in hand.

A wonderful aid to self-discipline is to practice delayed gratification. Think of a treat, whether this is an hour reading a book, listening to or making music, a bar of chocolate or glass of wine, a walk, or movie, or a catch-up phone call with a friend. Now, make a plan to reward yourself with this treat once the task is done. This motivates you to finish what you have started and helps you to feel good about yourself.

Energy is something that comes with feeling inspired. When you feel focused, no matter how busy you are or how hectic your life is, the energy will always be available to enable you to keep going. And the energy you put into accomplishing your goals goes out into the universe like a beacon that attracts more and more energy back to you. If you sit at home wishing, without getting out there and doing something to make it happen, it's unlikely to happen. But if you put energy out in the form of ideas, thoughts and, most of all, action, you'll see results. Once you set things in motion, you may be surprised at how much energy you have.

Enthusiasm is feeling good about what you are doing, and where it is taking you. Enthusiasm is a great energy-raiser. It generates a sense of excitement, it motivates you, and it inspires those around you because it's highly infectious. If you're enthusiastic about your goal, nothing can stand in your way, because the energy you give out creates a vortex that draws others to you who are then touched by that energy and who want to help. If you feel half-hearted, that's the energy that will come back to you. By joyously proclaiming to yourself that this is what you want, that you're on the right track and loving every minute of it, your success is assured.

Rebellion is the ability to step out of the mind-set that insists you stay in the place others have designated for you.

Countless children, expressing their decision to be whatever they want to be, have their pure potential squashed in infancy by being told it's out of reach, or they're not clever enough, or it's too hard. Some never recover and continue to feel victimised or unfulfilled throughout life. Others have to work hard to overcome the conditioning of well-meaning but unsupportive adults. Autonomy and self-respect come when you can shake off the opinions of others and go your own way. I know a lot of people who actively decided to get out of the confinements of the accepted establishment by openly rebelling, by asserting that, despite others' opinions, they were talented enough, and gutsy enough, to achieve their goals - and they have. Standing tall in the true glory of who you are is often considered an act of rebellion in society, but it's what you were born to do. Dare to be different!

Having confidence in yourself and your abilities is vital. If you don't feel confident about what you are doing, who else will? Sometimes an act of sheer bravado will do when you're feeling a little nervous. When you're dealing with other people who you feel less confident around, or who appear to think they are 'better' than you, it can help to remember that, whoever they are, they still eat, sleep, use the toilet, and have hopes, fears, insecurities and dreams - just like you.

You can respect others who have achieved something that you admire, you can learn from them and look to them as examples to be inspired by, but always remind yourself that you are capable, with work and focus, of doing your own thing in your own way. If you feel enthusiastic about your goals, the confidence tends to follow naturally. If you are surrounded by people who are negative about what you are aiming for, perhaps it is an indicator for you to look at why this is, and to resolve the situation through facing the hidden issues behind it.

And it always helps to seek the company of kindred spirits who inspire you. Your ability to *feel* and explore what motivates you enables you to move forward with a spring in your step, to set your sights on your goals, and to achieve your purpose. If the right motivation is there, and the willingness to work with it, you can live your dreams from the perspective of your own unique purpose, and both you and the world will be the richer for it.

Reminder: Whatever you do and say has a motive behind it. Knowing and understanding that motive makes you more able to guide and direct the course of your life.

Question to ponder: What is the primary quality that motivates you?

EXERCISES

Exercise 1. Evaluation

Spend some time thinking about the answers to these questions, as they may not come immediately. Then write them down in your journal.

- What is your immediate goal?
- What would you like to achieve in a year, and five years?
- What gifts and skills can you use towards the attainment of this goal?
- What assets can you call on? These could be emotional, material, logical, or cooperative.
- How can you further develop these? What steps can you take now to realise your goal?

Exercise 2. Increasing self-esteem

When someone pays you a compliment, accept it with a smile and make no comment, justification or excuses. Make a note of any praise or compliments in your journal and tell yourself that you are worthy of them. Allow yourself to acknowledge your positive qualities. Focus on these.

MICHAEL EAVIS

INTRODUCTION TO MICHAEL EAVIS

Michael Eavis is the Founder and organiser of The Glastonbury Festival Of Performing Arts, which takes place at his home in Somerset, Worthy Farm. The festival is known worldwide for its incredible variety of talent, both musically and through various other areas of artistic expression. Michael is proud that the festival reflects all kinds of music, attracts big names in the music world, and is at the cutting edge where new talent is concerned. In this open and warm conversation, he discusses how the idea for The Glastonbury Festival came about, how it has developed, and where his tremendous qualities of motivation stem from.

MICHAEL EAVIS

The Glastonbury Festival came about at a time in my life when I was in some disarray. I had fallen in love with Jean, and I was married to Ruth and had three little children, and Jean had three children. It was a very chaotic time, because I'd had a very orderly, sensible life until then. But then the love thing took over really, and it knocked me about a bit.

So we just wandered into a Bath Blues Festival, and I had a flash of inspiration, like a flash of light - it just went 'whoosh' and I thought 'Of course! This is fantastic!' And it fitted in with my particular situation at the time - love songs in a very 'love' situation. And I thought 'This is it. This is something that I really have to get involved with'. So that was the moment that started it all. The Glastonbury Festival was a love connected thing - it sounds a bit corny, but there we are, it's true nonetheless, and I just couldn't wait to get on with it. So I got on the phone the next day, and phoned around scaffolders and bands, and there was already the farm for a perfect venue. And I've never looked back since.

But it was a long struggle, an eleven-year struggle before we got anywhere. So, perseverance is the thing. Once you get an idea, if you believe in it, then you have to persevere, and 10 or 11 years is, I think, a short lead-in time really. So, you need to be aware of that. Basically, you have to keep on, and on, and on, and you don't give up - you never give up, not as long as you can keep going. So that's the core - that's me. I'm just a Somerset farmer with a tradition of rather stoic qualities. In spite of the apparent craziness of what I was doing, I'm still quite stoic in that I believe in a certain amount of discipline about following a vision. You make sure that you do it properly, and you just wait until it comes right, and it *will* come right in the end. If what you are doing is true, is meaningful to you, has a purpose and feels 'right' in your heart; if there are no flaws in it then it will work. But you need to stick at it for a long time - you can't expect things to happen straightaway.

Over the next ten years we had several festivals. I kept bouncing back and it didn't work, so I bounced back again, and it didn't work again, and I bounced back. It had to work eventually. Because I knew it was 'right', I knew it was a good idea, I knew it was something that was eventually going to work, but I didn't know how long it would take. That's the quality you need, though. You need to stick at it, you need to be durable, and you need to persevere.

I think my Somerset farmer, yeomanry background has been quite helpful. Because if I'd been wandering around, I wouldn't have had a base to start with. Having a base and having land - we've been here for over 100 years - is very useful, because it gives you a sense of permanence. And you're not threatened by anyone else, because you have your own fields. I was ripe for it really - I had the farm, I had the base, I wasn't going to move anywhere, take drugs or drink and blow it all away by being silly. I knew I had to keep it all together, and I knew what I wanted to achieve. And in 1981 it suddenly worked and did so from then on. It seems easy now, but 1981 was a turning point, when suddenly people wanted to come, they were happy to pay because they felt they were getting good value for money. And it didn't need a subsidy, it didn't need anything from the government, or an Arts Council grant. It just worked on its own merit, which was what I really liked about it.

It was an organic development really. More people got involved, who brought their input to it. I thought that the rock festival idea was a bit too 'rock'n'roll''- big stages, loads of speakers and security. It was a bit bland, really. And I thought that here was a way to go forward with the same idea, but to bring in all sorts of different areas of entertainment. That grew organically. When we realised what people wanted to do, people who worked here, who had ideas, we all worked together. We developed the Green Field into the major thing that it is now - and that's almost entirely non-music. So, we were expanding and growing, developing all sorts of ideas, and we had a sense of where we were going, we could feel our way through. It didn't come from the top down, it came from the bottom up. Because all of these youngsters were coming and doing things - sculptors, stonemasons, weavers… people doing all sorts of things were coming up with incredible ideas. And it was their stuff, it wasn't really mine. I knew what I wanted to do, but I gave them the opportunity to do what they wanted, to have a little bit of space in which they could make some money and develop something pretty. A couple from France had a lovely little café. I said, "This is beautiful!", and they said ''Thanks so much for giving us the opportunity to do exactly what we want to do.' It's great, isn't it? I was praising them, and they were praising me. (*Laughs).*

So that's why the festival works. There's this incredible

feeling of involvement with people, along with mutual appreciation and respect. And as far as I'm concerned, that's the important thing. All my team leaders have to respect and trust each other, in order to truly co-operate. Because there's a lot of money involved, and there are huge budgets now. Trust and respect are necessary, because the budget is split into little bits over the whole site, and managing the whole financial thing is quite a nightmare in itself. You delegate, you trust; it's a huge act of faith, but it just works - every year it works! It's extraordinary. I never cease to be amazed about it.

There's so much out there, and everybody who comes in puts in their best energy, the most creative aspects of themselves. Every single person who works here does this - it's absolutely unbelievable. I find it miraculous really, the amount of dedication that all these people put into this event in order to make it work.

We have roughly 20 areas of entertainment, and they all have their management structure. But we do try to make sure that musically (and this is my job) we represent the most fashionable aspect of every area of music at the moment. That's really important, so that we're not fuddy-duddy, or stick-in-the-mud, back in the 70's or anything. So, it has to be state of the art music and theatre. It sounds a bit twee, but it's really important to be right on the cutting edge. Because the kids like that, and basically it's where we want to be, so that the people who buy tickets to come to the show know that they're going to get all the very latest, and are going to see the bands of the future before they get really big. They see the bands like Oasis and Radiohead play here first, before they hit the big time. So, it's very trendy, it's the place for people like the University kids to come, who know that they're going to see the cutting edge of music - and of fashion and art as well. We have an artist from Cornwall who works for us at the moment, and he's incredible. I went down to Cornwall to see him, had a chat with him, and we liked what he had to offer. He's been here two years, and he's a huge success now. So we pick all these people out, and whatever the area is, we see ourselves as being right at the cutting edge of youth culture.

When I saw Oasis first, I knew instantly that they were going to be one of the biggest bands in the world. And with Radiohead too. I don't think the ability to "know" is all that clever really, but I'm quite good at it. To me it's obvious. When I hear a band, I know exactly whether they're going to move forward or not. But occasionally I get it wrong. I actually turned down U2 once, which was an extraordinary blunder (*laughs*), so I don't always get it right (*more laughter*). I went down to Exeter University, and maybe it was a bad night or something, but it was an extraordinary blunder.

But usually I'm pretty good at it. That's important, because we want people from all over the country, all over the world, to know that at the Glastonbury Festival they will see the bands who are going to be the leaders in their field. If they're not now, they will be next year or the year after. So that's why people come, and they see everything, all the teeny-weeny little stages that you get people playing on, who will eventually become superstars.

I've been asked to advise some record companies on bands, and I said, "No way." I don't want to get involved with that, otherwise I'd be pushing bands that I have a financial interest in, and I don't like that. I like to do it purely on merit. I don't have any financial interest in bands, as such.

What inspires me the most is a sense of achievement. There's such a buzz when you achieve something. I'm just so excited about what I'm doing, and it's an incredible position to be in, to be doing something that you actually enjoy. It isn't like a job of work to me, really.

And I have the farm, of course, as well. I have a good base, and I can afford to take a few risks. It's a perfect situation, really - the solid farm situation that's gone on for centuries; cows, milk, cheese and everything. And then I have this great sideline, this great fun thing. So I'm exceedingly fortunate. But I did take loads of risks with it. I could have lost the farm at one stage, which was crazy really. It was seriously risky at one point.

I'm not a gambler as such. I don't like gambling, but I put the farm on the line two or three times, and I just managed to save it. Things I shouldn't have done really. But if I hadn't taken that risk, the festival wouldn't have happened, and I felt that I had to do it because I believed in the festival *so* much that I had to be prepared to lose the farm for it. I remember thinking 'This is slightly wicked' (*laughs*) because I knew the farm, my heritage, was so important to me, and all my family have been here for centuries. But incredibly, the gamble worked. There's a lovely feeling about succeeding. It's very exciting in itself. I run up Glastonbury Tor with joy when I feel that I've done something I'm pleased about.

Not all of the feedback is positive - I get a lot of negative stuff as well, of course. Sometimes it worries me, maybe more than it should. But it's not really just me (*laughs*). I'm obviously in the driving seat, I had the vision of it - but everyone else is doing it too. I'm talking about people who come from all over the world to do things here. A lot of people think it's all me doing the work, and that makes me feel slightly guilty.

But obviously I feel very pleased that people like it so much, and there's an incredible amount of appreciation. Out in the world, wherever I go, people say "Fantastic - the last festival was terrific!" It's so much appreciation, and that's really nice. To be appreciated on that scale is the best thing - better than anything else really. We went to France on holiday and there was a beggar on the street in Montpelier, who looked as if he was on his last legs. And he suddenly sprang to life, he leaped up into the air and said "Michael Eavis!" and I thought 'My God, he's got life after all' (*laughs uproariously*). I do like it.

I always think that maybe we'll take a year off. It's quite

nice that it doesn't have to be cast in stone that you do it every year come rain or shine. There are all the other gigs which will happen regardless. And we don't have to do it, we don't *need* to do it. It happens because we want to do it. And that's important as well. It's a good basis for it to work from.

Chapter 3
Dealing With Challenges

The road of life leads us uphill and downhill. We travel over metaphorical mountains, through ravines, along winding narrow paths, into confusing mists; through meadows, deserts, and lush green forests. Sometimes the way ahead feels clear, and we have a sense of where we are going. At other times there are unexpected twists and turns, no-entry signs, and dead-ends where we have to stop and reconsider our route. When boulders or landslides block our way forward, we have to decide whether we can clamber over them, find a space that creates a way through, or go around them.

The challenges we face in our journey through life are like these boulders. Some may feel insurmountable at first glance, but our navigation of them makes us stronger, hones our skills, and adds to our knowledge and wisdom. Some challenges can be viewed as positive, even exciting. They stretch us, give us something to rise to, to meet head-on, and that can be stimulating and exhilarating. Why else would some of us choose to sky-dive, go potholing, hurl ourselves out on a bungee jump, trek through the wilderness of unexplored aspects of the mind or of nature? Meeting the challenges that we *choose* in life, for fun or understanding, reminds us that we are alive, tests our resources, and pushes us beyond our known boundaries into fresh territory.

PRESSURE CREATES DIAMONDS

Diamonds are considered to be among the most precious and beautiful of the Earth's geological gifts. Yet they are created through the compression of carbon by the intense weight of layers of strata over millennia. It is only when we dig deep and bring them to the surface that we can admire their radiance, their endurance, the way they reflect the light when faceted and polished. Diamonds can cut through substances that would be unscathed by other gemstones, so can be used as tools as well as being admired for their visual appeal.

Dealing with challenges creates human diamonds of each of us. We learn to find our own inner radiance and shine more brightly through confronting our fears. We grow in strength and confidence, cultivate the wisdom of experience, and develop tolerance, empathy and compassion towards ourselves and others. We learn to delve beneath the surface in order to discover the treasures within. The sense of accomplishment and increased confidence that results from resolving difficulties teaches us that we are stronger and more resourceful than we thought we were.

FACING FEARS

The fear of making mistakes can lead us to avoid situations that put us 'on the spot' or challenge us by stretching our abilities beyond the comfort zone. Our egos get caught up in an illusion of being in control, and that illusion inhibits us. Ultimately there *are* no mistakes. Whether or not we succeed in the way we imagined or hoped we would, we learn something from the experience. We grow. The decision to face our fears, accept the challenge, and take a leap allows us to break down barriers and boundaries within ourselves, and opens our minds to new possibilities.

Sometimes we can meet the challenges of life head-on,

confident that we can access past lessons and new insights and put them to constructive use. At other times, our fear of failure creates a form of paralysis that blocks the solution. Our *attitude* towards obstacles, difficulties and challenges can either lead us through them, or leave us feeling crushed and overwhelmed; at an impasse.

ACTION AND REACTION

In every moment of our lives we have a choice which is determined by our attitude at the time. How we *react* is determined by our attitude towards the situation, and our responses in that moment. If we are feeling low in confidence, lacking in self-esteem, or negative, any obstacles seem insurmountable and we feel like giving up. If we are feeling strong within ourselves, determined, inwardly calm and centred, or positive, we can put our energy to good use and work constructively towards a solution. Our attitudes can shift from day to day, depending on what mood we are in, and what our circumstances are. Our mood strongly affects our perception, and what may seem difficult on one day can be tackled with vigour on another.

THE TRAP OF ATTACHMENT

If we are in a state of emotional insecurity, fragility or fearfulness, and something blocks the way forward, we find it hard to cope. The outcome we desire takes on added significance. We feel in those moments that we *need* this particular outcome, that our lives cannot be happy or complete unless we attain it. Our neediness creates fear that these needs will not be met, and forges attachments that block a successful resolution. At this time, we can ask ourselves "How can I release this attachment? How can I open myself to receive the guidance or direction I need?" By releasing the *attachment* to a particular outcome, and by opening ourselves to the possibility that all will be well, we realise that so long as we put in our best efforts, whatever results from this will add to our growth. This attitude enables us to flow with the energy of the challenge and opens up a way through. If we relax and stop worrying, often the resolution appears effortlessly. We cease to be intimidated by fear, doubt or self-castigation if matters don't turn out as we hoped or planned.

When we try to control circumstances that are beyond our control, we suffer. As soon as we see that control is not working, and we relinquish the need for it, we relax and become more open to allowing creative solutions to come to us. Sometimes there is no choice but to 'let go' and allow the situation to work its own way through. With difficult challenges, often when you have pushed, striven, racked your brains, explored every resource available and still you feel 'stuck,' there comes a moment when something shifts. You come to a point where you know inwardly that enough is enough. Your inner sense of purpose prompts you to stop, and at that point you 'let go' spontaneously. You cease to battle it out because the energy to keep pushing dissipates.

This happens of its own accord because you cannot 'force' yourself to 'let go'. It just happens. The shift occurs. Where a moment ago you were filled with fear, anxiety, apprehension, frustration, suddenly an empty space appears. And into that space comes a feeling of acceptance, followed (often swiftly) by the solution, or the understanding of what the situation is about.

BREAKTHROUGH

Situations can also arise in which your common sense is telling you to give up. And you feel exhausted and *want* to give up, but your inner purpose prods you to keep going; to persevere, hold on, hold out, hang on in there. Then suddenly the breakthrough comes, and the solution appears. This could arrive through help or suggestions from a friend or acquaintance, where an insight into the situation becomes clear, or when you realise that the logical approach isn't working, and you can better solve the problem through lateral thinking. Wisdom is the ability to listen to your inner voice, your intuition, and to act on it. Through this comes mastery; the ability to accept what *is*, to do your best, and grow and learn through the experience.

Sometimes all that is needed is an alternative path. You may find a way around the obstacle instead of climbing over it or trying to break it down with a mental pickaxe. If you feel continually blocked at a certain point on your path, stop for a while and consider the situation. What is going on under the surface? What have *you* brought to the situation? How much of it is created by you and solvable by you, and how much of it is due to outside influences? What seems to be the lesson? Does this feel like a pattern? Have you come up against something similar in the past, and if so, how did you resolve it? Or is it an unresolved issue that is confronting you once again? If you see a pattern to this situation, how can you work creatively to break this pattern? It can help to ask yourself what gifts this situation holds for you.

PRECONDITIONED RESPONSES

In *The Consciousness Revolution*, an illuminating dialogue between Ervin Laszlo, Stanislav Grof and Peter Russell, Grof suggests that we still carry within us the memory of the pain and trauma of birth, and that this colours our attitudes in the future. Often, we become trapped in the past without realising it. We repeat old outworn attitudes and responses that were set up many years previously as inner defences or a means of coping. How much of your responses to obstacles, challenges and difficulties is a result of your experiences or attitudes in the past? How have you been conditioned (or programmed yourself) to respond? And what have been your strategies for dealing with or avoiding conflict that haven't worked for you, yet are still repeated? If we are harbouring a deep-rooted, unconstructive or unhelpful pattern or attitude, we will find ourselves repeatedly faced by situations that challenge us to move beyond that way of thinking until we allow ourselves to break through.

THE GIFTS OF CRISIS

At certain points in our lives, challenges can escalate to become crises. Crisis points are calls to immediate, urgent action. They are like a strident alarm that insists it is time to 'wake up.' Crises appear when we have fallen deeply asleep to our inner needs. Our consciousness becomes aware of this and sets all the alarm bells ringing to force us to take notice and *do* something. The point of crisis arrives when we are *inwardly* ready to step into a fresh mode of thinking, being and acting. It leaves us no choice but to step into a new paradigm, however much we try to deny it or cling to old and outworn patterns.

Just as there can be a crisis point during a high fever, when your body teeters on the edge of the moment between annihilation and healing, so does a crisis in your outer life bring you to a time for transformation. Like a snake, you have to shed the old, outgrown skin, otherwise life becomes constricted and constrained.

The challenge of a crisis is the necessity to embrace change, in whatever form it takes. This ultimately is constructive. If the caterpillar refused to enter the cocoon, the butterfly could not be born. If the butterfly didn't have to struggle to emerge from the cocoon, its wings would not develop the strength that enables it to fly. During times of crisis, if we rise to meet the challenge, we allow ourselves to connect with our deepest, most powerful resources. We learn to focus, to concentrate our energy. Inherent in the destructive potential within a crisis are the seeds for new growth, the emergence of increased creativity, evolution, and empowerment. Moments of crisis are painful, but they contain within them the gifts of transformation and healing at a fundamental level.

An important aspect of dealing with challenges is to acknowledge what is happening and how you are feeling. If you are worried, afraid, anxious, desperate, frustrated, angry, rebellious, or feeling sorry for yourself, allow yourself to listen to those feelings, and observe what you can glean from them. Ask yourself what the worst-case scenario in this situation could be. Face the fear. Then open yourself to the emergence of the outcome or solution that is right for you at this time. Often, by dealing with the feelings around the issue, you gain an understanding of what lies behind the challenge, why it is present in your life, and how to deal constructively with it. Sometimes we just have to ask the right question for the solution to present itself, and it is our choice as to whether we are ready to ask the question, as the following story illustrates.

THE HEALING QUESTION

The medieval Arthurian legends tell potent stories of an age that continues to fire the imagination. The wealth of symbolic imagery within these tales lives on because the age of romance, which they encapsulate, has an enduring appeal. The heroes and heroines, villains, priestesses and magicians are all still alive and strong, embedded in the archetypal layers of the collective and individual psyche. We can still learn much from them. This is the story of Percival (sometimes called Parsifal) and the Fisher King. There are many layers to this tale, but we shall look at the relevance of asking questions that bear the potential for healing.

Percival grew up with only the company of his mother, in the shelter of the forest. Unknown to him, his father and brothers, all knights, had been killed in battle, and his mother's greatest fear was that he would suffer the same fate. So, she kept him ignorant of, and protected from, the ways of the world, sheltered by her side. She taught him that it was impolite to ask questions, in the hope of keeping him always innocent, ignorant and incurious. But no-one can remain a child forever, and the maturation process involves the pain of cutting ties.

One day, out alone in the forest, Percival encountered a group of knights on horseback. Never having encountered such men before, he thought they were angels and fell to his knees before them, but they raised him to his feet and told him rousing tales of King Arthur and his court, of chivalry and battles, of heroic deeds and the search for the Holy Grail. Instantly, Percival determined to become a knight. He said farewell to his heartbroken mother and journeyed in the direction of the King's court.

On his travels he had many wondrous experiences, but the conditioning of his childhood, his carefully ingrained innocence and naiveté, meant that his lessons were learned slowly at first. Eventually he came to a beautiful castle surrounded by a wasteland. He was welcomed in and offered the hospitality of the Fisher King who, unknown to Percival, was the keeper of the Grail. The King had a festering wound in his groin that would not heal and, because he was sick and the countryside was a reflection of its guardian, his land had sunk from a fertile place to a barren place of gloom and devastation.

The Fisher King sat beside Percival, and together they feasted. Though curious about his host's obvious illness, Percival remembered his mother's caution and remained silent. After their meal a strange procession took place before them. Three beautiful young women passed by. The first maiden carried a spear that dripped blood. The second held a platter (in some tales, a sword). And the third held aloft a radiant chalice – the Grail itself. Percival bit his lip and swallowed down the questions that rose within him, for fear of seeming impolite.

Later he slept, and when he awoke in the morning he was alone. All had vanished. Puzzled, he went on his way, not realising what an opportunity he had missed.

If Percival had asked the Fisher King, "What ails you?" or "What is the meaning of this?" or "Whom does the Grail serve?" the Fisher King and his land would have been healed, and Percival would have become the next keeper of the Grail. It was only many years later, after a wealth of experiences and the accumulation of wisdom that Percival, along with Galahad and Bors, came into contact with the Grail again, and the quest reached its culmination.

THE KEY TO THE QUESTION

One of the many messages within this tale is the need to ask the question that lies within us and holds the key to inner healing and transformation. How often are we reluctant to ask the question that can lead to a solution and increased wisdom - the question that is vital to our growth? Truly, the questions that burn within Percival, and all of us, is "What is the purpose of this? How can healing be accomplished?" We need to ask what is wrong, deep down, and find out how we can reach the solution through acknowledgement and the willingness to confront the issue at hand.

As children, we accept what others tell us and believe it is the truth. We see ourselves as we are reflected in the eyes of those around us, and often believe that the mirror of the Self that we look into must be faulty if it is not in accord with the opinions of those around us. The rebellion of puberty is often sparked through the inner need to seek out our own answers. Then, as adults, we find maturity through taking full responsibility for ourselves and our lives, through finding our own solutions, asking the right questions in order to discover the answers that we need to know. And these come from deep within ourselves. Many of the blocks we encounter are the results of our conditioning and the perceptions we formed of ourselves and the world, absorbed from the significant adults around us – who were also trapped within their own conditioning.

The breakthrough, the healing, comes through examining our conditioned responses, releasing any feelings of judgement or blame that are directed towards ourselves or others, and asking the questions, "How can this be healed? What can I learn from this? What is its gift?" By exploring what we can discover about ourselves through facing the challenges, we are able to move into them, through them, and beyond them.

WINNING THROUGH

Challenges are an integral aspect to life. We may not always welcome them, but we need them. Evolution comes through having to find fresh resources, new ways of dealing with situations. The maintenance of an open, enquiring mind, and the trust that we are equal to the task, are the qualities that help to see us through and be grateful for what we have learned.

Some of the most successful people are those who have experienced tremendous disadvantages, drawbacks and obstacles. Yet they won through, and their lives provide a powerful source of inspiration to others. The qualities they have in common are ones that we all possess and can develop further.

The art of **perseverance** is the ability to keep going even when the odds feel stacked against you. This is motivated by the feeling that the goal is worthwhile and can be reached through dogged determination and tenacity. If you *really* want what you are aiming for, you will not be put off easily, because an inner prompting will keep spurring you onwards. If you are not willing to persevere, the questions to ask are, "Do I really want this? How *much* do I want this?"

Resilience is the ability to bounce back when your plans appear to be falling apart. It's the quality that you can call on in order to regroup yourself, decide on the action that is needed, and either dive back in, or start afresh with a different approach.

Determination to succeed is sometimes interpreted as ambition. However, this is not ambition in the cold sense of being willing to step on others to get to the top of the ladder. When you are facing challenges, determination essentially keeps you going, and helps you to hold your vision in your mind and heart even in times of struggle.

Acquiescing, or allowing others to make your decisions for you, leads to feelings of disempowerment and encourages you to hand over responsibility for your life to other people. This does not facilitate the development of inner strength or foster the growth process. Therefore, a certain degree of rebellion is necessary when you are feeling pressured. If you are willing to stand alone and you refuse to be caught up in the status quo, you gain the inner strength to stay with, and express, your sense of purpose.

When the challenges you face seem overwhelming, it is essential that you find and maintain your balance, your inner centre. This helps you to stay calm, and to *feel* your way ahead. If you listen to what your inner voice, the wise aspect of yourself, is telling you, the way forward becomes clearer. You will be able to sense when it is time to move on, when to persevere, and when to 'let go,' especially if you allow yourself to willingly accept the challenges and work with them rather than against them. When you are centred within yourself, you will know when to hold the space you are in while you patiently wait for the resolution, and when to retreat and find another route to your goal.

The times when we are dealing with challenges are the times when we are most in need of a positive attitude. It can be hard to believe in yourself and your ability to accomplish your aims when the way ahead seems blocked or unclear. Yet this is when you most need to remind yourself that you know you can do it. Being positive about yourself, acknowledging your achievements so far, and believing in your abilities helps to generate the energy you need to climb the highest mountain and explore the deepest caverns. And at the other side, an awesome landscape awaits you – the terrain of the wild, untrammelled Self; the discovery of the inner freedom that results from following your purpose.

Reminder: Challenges are opportunities that provide new ground for developing your strengths.

Question to ponder: What challenges have you already overcome? Which are you facing now?

EXERCISES

Exercise 1. Winning through

Look back over your life at times in which you have faced a major challenge. List these in your journal. Then answer these questions for each situation.

- What was it?
- How did you feel when you encountered it?
- What course of action did you take?
- What did this lead to?
- How did you feel afterwards?

What did this teach you about yourself?

Exercise 2. Facing Fears

In your journal, write down your fears. These could be general or specific. Focus initially on the fears that are directly related to a situation that you are currently dealing with. Now take a close look at these fears and write down what you feel has created them.

- Have you encountered these fears before?
- Are they part of a reactive pattern?
- How have you dealt with them in the past?
- What is the worst-case scenario that could have resulted?
- Did this scenario actually come about?

Often, our fears are illusory. Confronting them lessens their power over us.

Exercise 3. Unexpected outcomes

In your journal, note any situations in which you focused on a specific outcome that turned out differently to your hopes at the time.

- What happened?
- What was the eventual outcome?
- What did this lead into?
- Looking back at that time, can you see that outcome as positive, even though it was not what you had anticipated?

Exercise 4. Acknowledging strengths

In your journal, list all of your strong points. Add to these, as you may find that when you are low in confidence, you focus on weaknesses rather than strengths.

- When have you called these strong aspects of yourself into play?
- What resulted from this?
- How did you feel afterwards?

- Did anyone else recognise this in you, and comment on it?

Remind yourself of your strengths frequently, especially in moments when you feel disempowered.

Exercise 5. Sleep-solving

If the solution to a problem seems elusive, write it down on a piece of paper before you go to sleep. Place this under your pillow. Then relax and release any worries. Often the answer will come over the next two or three days.

This is where the term 'sleep on it' comes from. There is no magic involved – you are allowing your subconscious mind to find the answer and to bring it to the attention of the conscious mind.

WILLARD WIGAN

INTRODUCTION TO WILLARD WIGAN MBE

Willard Wigan, who was awarded an MBE in July 2007, is acknowledged as the greatest micro-artist the world has known. His sculptures are smaller than a speck of dust, so tiny that many of them are invisible to the naked eye, and they have to be observed through a powerful microscope. Willard's work inspires awe and a sense of the miraculous in all who view it, and it attracts vast numbers of visitors. Looking at the extraordinary detail and craftsmanship in these microscopic sculptures brings the realisation that creativity has no boundaries; the seemingly impossible is more possible than we realise.

Willard's craft was conceived and developed through his traumatic experiences as a severely dyslexic child. What began as an attempt to cope with his anguish became a gift that is now recognised and applauded all around the world. You can find out more about Willard at https://www.willardwiganmbe.com/

WILLARD WIGAN

When I was five years old I had learning difficulties - I still have. I'm dyslexic. It wasn't diagnosed at the time. I started school in 1962, and dyslexia wasn't recognised then. They just classed me as illiterate and used to make an example of me by showing the kids my work and saying "Look how disgusting Willard's work is. If you don't listen to me, your work will be like his." So, they used to parade me round the whole school. From that, every little bit of confidence I had was gone. So, I hardly used to go to school. I'd go off into the woods and study all the insects, because insects fascinated me more than people because of the way they communicated. And they were small, but their cycle of life had a meaning. So when the teacher would say I was nothing, I knew there was no such thing as nothing - something always exists, you see. So, I knew I had *something*.

I started making little houses for ants and things - little merry-go-rounds, see-saws. Small things, with wood. And from there, I'd make microscopic tables and chairs, and put little bits of sugar on the table, and watch the ants come up and eat it. I got tied up in this small world, the world that people ignore, the world that people disregard as being nothing.

I did little sculptures of the teachers. They made me feel small, so I wanted to make them look small in my child's mind. You see, if you tell somebody of that age that they're no good, they become what you say they are. So, I became what they said - which made me paranoid, in a way. I felt that I needed to do something about it. So, I realised that small things often have the biggest impact. And I started making these little things to speak for me - so that I didn't have to speak any more. The work did the talking.

So, from there, I realised that what I had was different. I'd go home from school so excited, because I couldn't wait to go out into the woods to look at the ants. After that, I'd go home, into my bedroom, and I'd get little bits of broken glass and razor blades, and I started making these microscopic figures. At that time, you could see the shape, but I hadn't developed. This was the beginning; this was me saying to people "You make me feel small, but now I'm going to use small to show you how 'big' something really is." Everybody accepts something just because they can see it - why not accept something you can't see? Why should something be a certain size to be appreciated? So, I kept seeing these small things that were happening. I'd give someone a small present, and I realised from their reaction that people liked small things - within reason, of course (*laughs*). From there, I noticed that all these small things were having an impact. And I thought that if I made my work even smaller, people would like it even more. But I never told anybody, because I was programmed to believe that everything I did was no good, and I believed that.

I continued making small things, but I was aware that it was demanding so much from me. I was breathing while I was doing it, and I realised that, in order to get smaller, I had to stop breathing. So, at the age of 6, I used to hold my breath, and I saw that it worked better, because I could control it. I could feel the pulse moving in my hand, which meant I had to squeeze my fingers to get even more control. Then I could feel my heart beating. So, I used to 'catch it' in between the heartbeats, do a stroke in between. There are thousands of strokes to a piece, and sometimes the glass would crush, and fragments would break off. Then I'd use a razor blade. Sometimes it would take me up to 9 or 10 hours. At that time, I did a carving of King Kong, as a little tribute to him. I had a fixation for King Kong, I felt sorry for the way they took him away, in captivity, brought him into so-called civilisation, and killed him. That carving was on the top of a cocktail stick. But it was just for me - no-one ever saw it.

Years passed on, and I left school with nothing, not even my 11 Plus. I went to work in a factory, chucking little bits of metal into a container, got my wages, and thought, "At least I'm alive". But all that time, I hardly used to go out. I'd stay in my bedroom, making things. I'd go to model shops and buy little Swann Morton craft blades and develop what I was doing.

Because of the difficulty of the small things I was making, I realised that it would be easy for me to do big things. When I was 30, I did a carving - a portrait of a friend's mum. She liked the carving and bought it. People started coming to me, and I began to make a living from woodcarving. Then I worked in a Community Centre, teaching woodcarving. From there, everybody was telling me that I was good. That gave me the encouragement I needed. So, I continued to do the big sculptures, and ignored the small ones - no-one had seen them yet; nobody knew about them. Then I was happy, because I was doing something that I could do naturally. No-one taught me - I could just do it.

Time moved on to 1999. I'd continued to do the big stuff, because I was doing exhibitions, and winning awards. People were commissioning me. I felt wanted, it felt really good. People praised my work. Prince Charles saw the carving that I did of the Queen Mother and was overwhelmed. I was in the newspapers, and people were talking about me. But no-one knew about the small things, until Prince Edward and Sophie were getting married. Then I decided to do a carving of the two of them on a match, and I called it 'the Perfect Match'. I showed it to a friend, and he told the newspapers. Then everybody got excited and said "Wow! How the hell did he do that?" I opened the newspapers, and there it was. So, I thought, "This is nice, everybody likes what I do." Then everyone was asking how I managed to carve on a matchstick - but a matchstick is huge in comparison to what I carve, anyway. Most of the things I carve can't be seen with the naked eye.

I thought this was great. I'd been doing all these cocktail stick carvings for years. Then, all of a sudden, 'The Big Breakfast' show phoned me up, and I was on the show. People started talking about my small work, more than the big work. This felt great, because now I felt I wasn't wasting my time. From being on television, I had a lot of phone calls from people, and Ultimate Art Limited was one of them. One lady wanted me to exhibit my work in her house (*laughs*).

Before 'The Big Breakfast' show, I did an exhibition in Birmingham City Centre. I did a carving of an angel. While I was carving the angel, a lot of people were looking at me, saying "Oh, you're the one that was in the newspapers. You did that small sculpture. How did you manage to do that?" And I felt really good, because people were telling me now that I was good. And I believed it for the first time in my life.

Then I noticed that there was a dragonfly flying around. People were nervous of it. I watched it as it flew around in a circle and landed on my angel. Then I folded the wings back gently, took it to the entrance of the shopping centre, and set it free. I went back to the carving, and a while later someone called my name from across the floor. It was this lady, 60ish, and she asked if I remembered her. I didn't, until she said "Do you remember my son? I'm Adrian's mum." Then I remembered her. He'd died, aged 17, in the Falkands war. A tragic waste of life.

She asked if I'd do a carving of Adrian for her. We used to play together as kids, and I'd catch dragonflies for him. She was wearing a brooch with a dragonfly on it. And a dragonfly had been in there, just hours before. The dragonfly is very significant to me. In New York, they exhibited my Statue of Liberty in the eye of a needle, within the real statue. We were in downtown New York. What did we see flying around, but a dragonfly - in the city centre. You don't get dragonflies in those areas, just as you don't get them in shopping centres in the middle of Birmingham! It seems that, wherever I go, dragonflies appear. What's more, I don't sign my work with my name - I carve a little dragonfly instead.

Well, this lady asked me to do a carving of her son, so I asked for a photograph. She carried one all the time, but it was badly faded. I didn't know if I could do it without a 3D image. So, I asked her to bring her husband over and she did. And I got them both to turn sideways, and backwards, and combined their features and carved him. And it looked exactly like him. She cried when she saw it.

Afterwards, people were asking me to carve their grandmothers, dogs, cats, everything. I was inundated with portrait sculptures, and I felt overwhelmed and unable to cope. I used to lie awake at night, praying for help. My prayers were answered, and I was rescued when I met up with Alan Devy and

Russell Merridew of Art International, who said “We’re currently setting up an exhibition in Bath, with a guy called Mike Watts. It’s going to be called ‘The Impossible Microworld’, and we’re exhibiting the work of Manuel Ussa”, who I’d never seen or heard of. And they invited me to be part of it. I thought it sounded interesting. They rang, and came on the same day; sat down and told me everything they wanted to do. And it was everything that I wanted to do, the synchronicity was all there. I noticed while we were talking that we had the same things in common, we liked the same things. It was just meant to be.

From there, we developed a good relationship, and I went on to be managed by Ultimate Art Ltd., who owned my work and promoted its exhibition. People are mystified by how small my work is. I know now that I can carve the smallest sculptures on earth. My work has taken a new turn. Now I can carve on a human hair, on a speck of dust, a granule of sugar. I can carve, in detail, things that cannot be seen with the naked eye. My skills have improved. I can keep still for 22 hours without moving. Now I’m being appreciated, accepted, recognised - not for being dyslexic, but for who I am as a person, and for my skills. Now surgeons, scientists, people are mystified by what I can do. But this work is so physically demanding - it’s hard to conceive just how hard it is.

To explain it, it’s like trying to pass a pin through a bubble without the bubble bursting. This micro-art is even harder than that. It’s so hard, you end up crying. You feel like giving in, because it puts you through so much pain. The worst time I ever had with it was when I was doing the tall ship on a granule of sugar. I was rigging the ship with spiders webbing, with a pin that I’d ground down *so* fine. I tried to pull the rigging over the top of the sails, onto the mast, but I got distracted and lost my concentration. The webbing wrapped itself around the mast and I tried to retrieve it without pulling everything off. Eventually pieces ended up stuck to my fingers and the whole sculpture was obliterated. After 2 months work!

But now, I go into retreat to work. I go away to Jersey and live as a recluse for 2 months, to work peacefully.

It's hard work, but I will continue to do it, because people like what I do, and I like them liking what I do. Small things mean so much, and they can say a lot. It doesn't matter what we see. Sometimes we see things in a different perspective. Because we don't understand the world that's beneath our feet. Science has shown us for years that there's another world - but we disregard it because we can't see it. But when we do, we're knocked out by it. When you look at my work, without a microscope or magnifying glass, you won't see anything. But it's there!

I didn't use magnification at all until 1998. The toothpick sculptures, and everything before that time, was done with the naked eye. Then I realised that the work was going to get smaller so I decided to use magnification. But even though I do that, it still means I have to have a steady hand, and nerve control. I warm up for 2 hours or more, by keeping my hands still. Then I'll start carving. I can stay in the same position for 22 hours at a time, I slow down my heartbeat and breathing, and work in the spaces between. Sometimes, I feel as if I'm the same size as the piece that I'm working on. I've 'gone down' to that scale. At other times, I feel as if my hands are being held or guided - I'm not consciously aware of making the movements myself. Sometimes I feel a presence.

I have very vivid dreams. I've often dreamed I'm in Egypt, in a field, and I have a big piece of wood. I'm carving away, and people give me water and fruit. It's always in this specific place. I remember looking through a book on Egyptology, and there was a sculpture that was almost identical to the one that I was doing in the dream. It made me feel strange.

To achieve this type of work, you have to have incredible patience. People are shocked when they see the work. They cannot conceive of it. We've had people walk into the exhibition who have stood there for hours, open-mouthed. Sometimes they don't want to leave. Sometimes they think it's a trick. It's like being taken into another dimension, another world.

I have now carved a ship on an eyelash. A girl in the eye of a needle. A village on a speck of dust - with trees and everything. I've done a cottage with a garden on a pin-head; a camel in the eye of a needle; Samson splitting a human hair - where you get a split end in a human hair, I've carved Samson in between that, splitting it, in perfect detail. His muscles, beard, loincloth. I've done Stuart Little in the eye of a needle; Adam and Eve on a pencil head; Goldilocks and the three Bears on a toothpick. And Elvis Presley in the eye of a needle (*laughs*), my mother in the eye of a needle. I've made things so small that you can't see them with the naked eye, but they're in perfect detail.

I'd like the world to see my work. I've taken it to a level that nobody understands. Even technology is shocked. I'm going to take it further still. Because what was done to me, being made to feel small, has made me greater. So even though it's hard and painful to do this work, I continue. I am the world's greatest micro-miniaturist, and that's what I'm going to maintain. And I haven't *begun* to get *really* good yet - there's more to come.

Chapter 4
Evolution

While we are engaged in connecting with our sense of purpose, we traverse previously unexplored terrain within ourselves. We shine light into the caverns of the deep self, widen our horizons, and discover that we are only limited by our *belief* in limitation. We shift perspective, grow, and look back in surprise at how much we have changed along the way. A revolution takes place within us as we cast off old ideas, outworn patterns of thinking, and ways of being and behaving that have ceased to be useful. We begin to observe an evolution occurring that takes us from a limited view of the self to an inner sense of our connectedness with the vast story of life that we are part of, and party to.

Life is a continually evolving process. From the first spark that precipitated the birth of the universe to the formation of dust clouds, stars, galaxies, planets, and the vast array of life-forms over aeons of time, evolution is ongoing. Species emerge, develop, and some disappear, leaving traces of their passing, while we back-track into their worlds, and attempt to fast-forward from our era into an unknown future.

Our nature as human beings is to question, to continually fan the flames of curiosity that keep us searching for answers, and for the meaning within those answers. The motivating force is the desire to know, to understand, to delve into the deepest mysteries in order to illumine our own minds and pave the way forward for future generations.

ONE AND ALL

When Charles Darwin wrote *On the Origin of Species,* humankind eagerly leaped on board the adventure in order to set off for the new shores and map the uncharted landscape. The idea of our species evolving as a logical progression was initially shocking and then very appealing, and for a while appeared to overrule the necessity for a Creator. In the womb, we evolve from the miraculous union of egg and sperm, becoming amphibian, gradually developing into human form. We carry within us the blueprints of other species, other creatures, and the stuff of stars. The recent scientific discoveries are once more opening up the discussion of the existence of an intelligence that underlies all forms. The search for what breathes life into the cosmos continues, fuelling an ever-increasing plethora of discoveries and hypotheses.

What makes each of us different? What makes us unique? The common denominator of all life is vibration. Each of us experiences the differentiation between ourselves and others as a slight fluctuation in vibrational resonance. Each organ in our bodies is tuned to a particular frequency, and our bodies as a whole hum to their own special tune. The understanding of this is accelerating the emergence of new methods of healing. Sound healing employs tones that harmonise with the parts of ourselves that are 'out of tune.' Colour therapy improves the vibrational balance through employing the various frequencies in light that have specific effects. Systems such as homeopathy distil the vibration of substances that in full-scale doses could be harmful, and then dilute them until the original material substances cannot be detected. The vibrational effects on the body stimulate healing.

Everything in existence is created through vibration. An atom, an ant, a human, a planetary or stellar body all resonate to their own vibratory pitch and pattern. And, like a musical note in a symphony, each vibration is linked with all others to create unimaginably complex music that reverberates through the cosmos. Our inner being exists in a harmonic resonance with the whole because, in essence, we are created from the same matter. Life emerges from a singular state. The creative force of the universe expresses itself through the myriad forms of creation.

QUANTUM EMERGENCE

Initially, physicists considered the smallest component of the universe to be in the form of a point. This evolved through to Newtonian physics, then to the realisation that extraordinarily small packets of energy could be observed as either a particle or a wave, depending on the perspective of the observer. The name 'quantum' derives from the term 'quanta,' meaning 'a packet of energy.' More recently, the developments in theoretical physics have evolved into the superstring theory, among others. This could facilitate the longed-for marriage between the macrocosm of general relativity and the microcosm of quantum theory, through the hypothesis that the building blocks of life consist of tiny strands curled up within themselves. The rates at which they vibrate determine the forms that take shape. The music of the cosmos is contained within all and is played out in a continual symphony, with individual instruments entering and leaving the show as evolution shifts and moves on.

The 'theory of everything' that string theory appears to encapsulate could possibly explain the nature of the basic components of creation. However, the extraordinary symmetry, diversity and beauty of the evolving cosmos that blossoms from the genesis of a single mathematical equation cannot merely be viewed in simple, reductionist terms. A symphony is composed of many notes, many vibrational tones in an orchestra of widely differing instruments. Yet the knowledge of this does not detract from the pleasure we feel when we hear the music; it adds to it. The questions about *what* the universe is formed of may be on their way to being answered, but the scientific answer to *why* it exists is still open-ended.

HOLOGRAPHIC IMAGES

Here is a possibility worth musing on. What if the universe is a conscious being, experiencing itself through each aspect of its own creation? What if, through the lens of each form that exists, the universe can become conscious of itself? That consciousness could have existed before the Big Bang that birthed our known universe. We could each envision ourselves as the sensory organs of creation, experiencing our own perceptions so that we can further understand ourselves and the nature of life, in order for the universe to experience and understand it*self*.

The theory of implicate order described by physicist David Bohm implies that the universe could be like a hologram. We see the apparently separate outward forms, yet within everything there also rests a fractal image in which the whole of the universe is encoded. The purpose of each of us is part of the purpose of the whole. The images of the Mandelbrot set, beautiful fractals in gloriously vibrant colours, adorn a multitude of greetings cards and posters and have contributed to a widespread realisation of the beauty and complexity of life, illustrating the mystery and perfection of the whole as more than the sum of its parts.

CREATIVE CONSCIOUSNESS

In the question of our place in the scheme of things, the issue of whether or not we have free will arises. Could it be that the connection with the Infinite, while present within us, allows us through its unconditional nature to direct the course of our lives, in order to grow and evolve?

Evolution is the perfect tool for creating through consciousness. Our consciousness is greater than the sum of the information contained in our DNA, or in the ability of our brains to be microprocessors. Our minds and our consciousness are more than the basic genetic blueprint that is encoded in our bodies. As we become more self-aware, we realise that the deeper we delve into life's mysteries, the more questions arise, and the more we perceive the gargantuan scale of possibilities.

THE MIND/BRAIN DILEMMA

Scientific studies into the significance of near death experiences (NDE's) have been raising some potent questions about the nature of consciousness. Dr. Sam Parnia is the chairman of the Horizon Research Foundation, a charity that aims to support scientific research into NDE's. His study, the first of its kind in Britain, reveals that between 6% and 12% of patients in the UK and Europe who have 'died' during a heart attack have clearly described, in detail, their witnessing of events leading to their resuscitation. During this interval they were considered clinically dead, with no evidence of pulse, respiration or electrical activity in the brain. Yet their thought processes appeared to carry on, during the time that the body was not functioning. The initial hypothesis that the out-of-body experiences reported by some of the patients were caused by hallucinations due to lack of oxygen to the brain have now been discarded. The patients' awareness of the events taking place during their resuscitation is a strong indicator that consciousness exists independently from the brain; that it is a separate entity in itself. Dr. Parnia's research, described in his own words in his interview in the next chapter, is leading in the direction of scientific proof of the existence of the 'soul' and of the continuation of consciousness after the death of the physical body.

The nature of consciousness itself is the mystery that has fuelled the greatest thinkers and philosophers over the ages.

The answers are there, waiting for us. Our survival as a species is dependent on our ability to evolve, to change, to move forward through the incorporation of new discoveries and insights. The path leads deeper into the journey towards a more profound understanding of our minds, of human nature, and its contribution to the web of life that enfolds us. As Peter Russell reminds us at the conclusion of *Chapter 1*, the common thread of humanity is the knowledge that we are self-aware. This self-awareness holds the potential for a state of universal awareness, in which our consciousness is expanded to the recognition that we are inextricably connected to the whole.

QUIET EVOLUTION

Our challenge in that quest lies in the ability to be open-minded, to continually question, and to follow our gut-feelings and our intuition. Some of the greatest insights have sprung from inner musings while in a relaxed, receptive state. The theory of gravity emerged from Newton's observation of an apple falling from a tree. The theory of relativity was inspired by Einstein's fantasy of riding on a beam of light. Friedrich Kekule's discovery of the shape of the benzene molecule in 1864 was inspired by a dream-vision, in which a snake was biting its own tale. For each of us, the quiet moments are the times when a mental lightning bolt strikes and changes our perception irrevocably. The gift from Consciousness can then be taken up, developed, and communicated. Without these moments, without the allowance of the exploration of inner space, our progress would be slowed or halted, and atrophy and stagnation would set in. Evolution is the process of further developing what 'works,' what can survive, while releasing the forms that are no longer equipped to carry on.

THE IMPORTANCE OF CURIOSITY

We see this constantly in everyday life. Ideas emerge and are developed or discarded. Goals change. Relationships shift and evolve or are left behind. Our minds, if constantly focused, hone and sharpen themselves so that we are more able to grasp concepts. Being open to new ideas creates a continual state of expansion, as each fresh idea gives rise to yet more. We are a curious species, and that curiosity is our tool for inner growth, outer development, and the evolution of consciousness into a more expanded knowledge of itself.

In an everyday sense, that curiosity constantly fuels our sense of purpose. It shows us numerous possibilities that can be explored, and it motivates us to sift through and follow the ideas that take us in the direction of our chosen goal. To be open to possibilities necessitates an urge to enquiry, and a belief that the answers are accessible. This paves the way to the ability to see, and act on, opportunities that arise which can further our development.

How much do you truly notice of what is around you? Much of our time can be frittered away in a half-sleep, a state of 'soft-focus' in which the edges of life are blurred and indistinct. If you have just been introduced to someone new, can you remember afterwards what colour their eyes are? What are the details of the place where you met them? The honing of our mental faculties involves being fully 'awake' and aware in each moment – being fully conscious. This enables us to be truly alive, vibrant, alert and interested in every facet of life. We become more open, which makes us more receptive to everything that takes place around us and within us. Our ability to notice small details, and the direction events are moving in, helps us to evaluate; to see where we are heading and how to arrive there, and to perceive the direction that current trends are moving in. This is useful not only in view of achieving your goals. It also encourages, through wakefulness and mindfulness, the allowance of the evolution process that is constantly taking place within ourselves.

ENTELECHY

The *entelechy* is the name given to our inner dynamic purpose. It is the seed of potential that nestles deep within us, containing the fractal image of who we truly are and what we can become. The Greek philosopher Socrates first coined the term entelechy, and the great mystic Teilhard de Chardin brought it to public attention. In her interview transcript in *Chapter 7*, Jean Houston explains the nature of her work in bringing the entelechy to the light of full consciousness in individuals through the auspices of The Foundation of Mind Research that was co-founded by Jean and her husband, Robert Masters.

The inner sense of purpose that is governed by the entelechy is the driving force behind our lives, helping us to blossom into the fullest expression of ourselves. It holds the key to the development of the skills and abilities that open the door to the perception of our inner purpose. The bright moments during which we are suffused with an inner *knowing* are illuminated by the promptings of the entelechy on the conscious mind. Our experiences of our connection with the entelechy are perceived when we feel a sense of unity, of one-ness; a feeling of the perfection of this precise moment and all it holds. It is the intrinsic sense of 'rightness,' the 'spring morning feeling,' the sensation of unspeakable delight underlaid by a deep inner peace. This both informs and enhances our everyday life and enables us to function at a level far beyond our so-called 'human' capacity.

The entelechy can be viewed as the landscape of the soul; the place where dreams and visions that lead to greater awareness are born; the home of the deep magical self. Whether or not we are aware of it, that seed of potential rests within us, awaiting the call to outward expression. Our true capabilities far exceed anything the mind, with its tendency to categorise and limit, can possibly imagine.

INTUITION

Central to our ability to connect with the entelechy is our intuition. The moments when we suddenly 'know' something are vivid, light-filled, inexplicable. The intuition is our inner guide, the aspect of us that takes away the crackle and static of all the wavelengths we constantly inhabit. It presents us with a fully formed, clear image that is pure, truthful and profound. It can appear in the guise of an insight, or a feeling that we may call a hunch, or as a clear directive which shows us the way ahead. If we take heed of, and follow, our intuitive impulses, they are invariably correct. And the more we tap into this aspect of ourselves and work with it, the more it develops within us because, like radios, we can attune ourselves to its frequency.

Following our intuition reminds us that there is a knowing within us that is more profound than our logical minds, and this shows us increasingly more possibilities for the full expression of our inner nature. The layers and levels encompassed by the intuition are reflected in the physical body (as a gut feeling), in the emotions (as a sensation of joy and rightness), in the mental aspect (as an inner knowing that cannot be disputed), and in the spiritual Self (as a feeling of complete unity). The more we allow this and flow with it, the more it reveals itself to us, until it is the central, most trusted aspect of our lives. The entelechy can then be felt and seen to burst forth from its seed, to emerge from its hidden core within the deep self, and to radiate in all its magnificence into the full light of being.

COMMUNICATION

The communication of one soul to another, one voice to another, spreads like wildfire to join with many other souls and voices, resonating onwards through the symphony of the universe that our physical ears cannot hear, but that our inner selves know and respond to. Our ability to communicate through our bodies, through speech, through the written word, the hidden codes in symbols and mathematics, through telephones, radio, television and the internet, holds the facility for potent strides forward in our evolution. The human race is a species impelled by, and governed by, communication. Knowledge spreads swiftly, fear diminishes us, enthusiasm is wildly infectious. The insights of the few can become widely accessible to the many, both through traditional methods of communication and through our continual connection to what the biologist Dr. Rupert Sheldrake calls 'the morphogenetic field'.

Morphic resonance is Rupert Sheldrake's hypothesis of formative causation. It suggests that all self-organising systems are organised by 'morphic fields' which influence the processing of information from one system to another. These fields are non-material in nature, and they enable each of us to tap into the experiences of both our ancestors and those who live in our time. Morphic fields appear to act as collective information banks, which could explain similar discoveries being made simultaneously on different continents across the world. Shifts in consciousness in small groups of individuals can also facilitate similar shifts in other groups around the world, if those people are open to expansion. The fabric of life that we are woven into has many strands and many dimensions.

At our present stage of evolution, we face a choice. We can continue to follow the old ways of greed, antagonism and separatism, and subsequently put at great risk not only our own species but also many other life-forms on this planet. Or we can choose to discover why we are here, what we can contribute to each other, and to the whole, through embracing co-operation, understanding, and increased wisdom. Our interconnectedness implies that what affects one also affects many. The reverberations of humanity's influence on this one small planet are felt across the universe as ripples in the finely tuned conduction of the music of the cosmos. Our way ahead comes through the decisions of individuals, who each influence other individuals, to connect with their inner source of love, inspiration, inner knowing, and compassion.

Reminder: You are more than the sum of your experiences. You have your own unique part to play in the symphony of life.

Question to consider: Where do you see yourself heading within the next five years?

EXERCISES

Exercise 1. Music and emotion

Think of a particular song that affects you deeply.
How do you feel when you hear it?
Does it send a shiver up your spine, or elevate your mood, or provide the energy for you to accomplish a task?
Pay close attention to what it is in that song that resonates with you. Music sets up a set of vibrations that attunes you to your emotional self.

Exercise 2. Special quality

In your journal, write down one quality within yourself that shines out beyond all others. What is your special quality? Is it love, compassion, intelligence, perception, inquisitiveness, nurturing, strength, resilience, or something else? Imagine that part of your purpose is to develop and embody that quality. How can you work with this? What results are possible through this?

Exercise 3. Opening to insights

Set aside a few minutes regularly, perhaps once a week, when you allow yourself to relax and drift off. In your journal, note down any ideas and insights that result from this. See where these threads lead to.

Exercise 4. Relaxed awareness

Practice being awake and alert. During a conversation, mentally note everything about the people around you – hair and eye colouring, body language, tone of voice, clothes. Try this exercise at work, or at a party. Afterwards, see how many details you can remember. You can learn a great deal about other people through observation.

NOTE: The trick is to be relaxed, while paying attention. Very little effort is required. After a while, you will find that this occurs automatically.

Exercise 5. Random joy

Each time you experience that 'spring morning feeling,' the sheer joy of being alive, fully immerse yourself in it. Note down in your journal the time and circumstances in which it arose. Was this precipitated by anything? Can you repeat that feeling consciously?

PETER ULRICH

INTRODUCTION TO PETER ULRICH

Fans of cult musicians Dead Can Dance and This Mortal Coil will be familiar with Peter Ulrich as the percussionist for the former and a contributor to the latter. A multi-talented composer and musician in his own right, Peter's solo albums reflect a diversity of cultural and musical influences. Although some tracks point to an ongoing affinity with Dead Can Dance, there is also a combination of genres which are unique to Peter and mark him out as an adventurous musician with a gift for creating an intriguing array of moods and themes.

His first album, *Pathways and Dawns* (Projekt), garnered reviews which compare him favourably with Brian Eno, Depeche Mode, Syd Barrett, John Cale and Dead Can Dance. Medieval, ethnic and folk influences are lifted up beyond their roots, developed through the inclusion of electronic instruments, and skim the borders of rock, pop and gothic. Brendan Perry of Dead Can Dance arranged, recorded and produced six of the eight tracks on Pathways and Dawns.

Enter The Mysterium (City Canyons Records) is Peter's second album. It's dark and mysterious, explorative and compellingly haunting, with a rich combination of medieval, ethnic and electronic instruments. Each song comprises a story within a story, with themes culled from the context of the extensive library collection of 16th century doctor, John Dee. The track *Through Those Eyes* features both of Peter's daughters. The Scryer and the Shewstone, which is also on the award-winning *John Barleycorn Reborn* album (Woven Wheat Whispers and Coldspring Records), has an up-tempo melody which complements the depth of the lyrics, while *The Witch Bottle of Suffolk* is a forbidding tale that brings to mind the witching hour and Hallowe'en.

In this interview, originally conducted in March 2008, then updated in November 2018, Peter talks about his work in the context of his early influences, his connection with Dead Can Dance, and the stories behind his solo albums.

Peter Ulrich's albums are available through HMV, Play, Woolworth, Tesco and CD Baby, and at the following websites:
http://www.themysterium.info/
http://www.citycanyons.com/ulrich/index.html

PETER ULRICH

I was a child in 60's London, so my earliest influences would have been the obvious groups and artists of the time - The Beatles, Rolling Stones, The Who, Bob Dylan, Elvis, the great Tamla Motown era, and so on. My parents were avid radio listeners so I was also exposed to a lot of light and mainstream classical music, and my aunt Barbara was an operatic choral singer who was in many 'west end' musicals which I loved being taken to, especially when I got the opportunity to go backstage.

The first single I ever bought was 'Urban Spaceman' by the Bonzo Dog Doo Dah Band, and the first album was a hits collection by The Move. The first band I formed (age 11) was called The Vibrations (after the Beach Boys' 'Good Vibrations') and the first song I can remember writing was called 'Cuckoo Hill' which totally ripped-off Donovan's 'Jennifer.'

In the early 70s I was into Ziggy Stardust era Bowie, followed by getting heavier with a Deep Purple phase. By the age of 14 or so, I was rejecting the mainstream commercial charts music and searching for greater stimulation. I found this in progressive rock which, at that time, was the obvious home of the white, middle-class teenage wannabe intellectual. So I immersed myself in Genesis (strictly Peter Gabriel era only!), Pink Floyd (including catching up on the Syd days that I'd previously missed) and then searched out the bands that became my real favourites of the era such as Nektar, Caravan and Man so that virtually all the other kids at school didn't have a clue what I was on about.

In the late 70s I was as thrilled as most anti-bland-pop people by the emergence of punk and the transition into the highly fertile 'new wave' era that followed and gave rise to so many influential bands that I couldn't begin naming them, with the exception that I always loved Talking Heads and the creativity of David Byrne. I also got into reggae - the harder, underground political reggae - stuff like Steel Pulse, Misty in Roots, Linton Kwesi Johnson and (long before their awful pop reincarnation of later years) Aswad.

The turn of the 80s heralded the arrival of two huge influences - firstly the amazing sound of Joy Division, and secondly the release of the first WOMAD album alerting me to some of the extraordinary sounds which are now absurdly lumped together under that daftest of categorisations 'World Music'.

So it was with a mix of Joy Division on the one hand and Nusrat Fateh Ali Khan and The Burundi Drummers on the other floating around in my head that I first met Brendan Perry and Lisa Gerrard in 1982 and was invited to join Dead Can Dance which had just arrived from Australia minus a drummer.

The way these influences impacted on my joining DCD was simply that, without these reference points, I would have been too far removed from Brendan and Lisa's wavelengths to have been of any use to them. However, that's as far as it went. I did not contribute to the creation of the DCD sound - I was rather a VERY lucky participant in the performance. Everything about the DCD sound was created by Brendan and Lisa, and their ideas, their passion and their creative processes would become far and away the biggest influence on my future solo works.

It's difficult to say exactly how my early influences have impacted on my solo albums, but I've had comparisons drawn in reviews with Syd Barrett/early Floyd, John Cale, Alan Parsons and Peter Gabriel. One review of my first album even called it the album The Beatles would have made had they signed to 4AD rather than Capitol, so I guess those early influences must be all wrapped up in there somewhere.

I never had an ambition to be 'a musician'. I just wanted to be involved in music - listening, writing, playing - whatever and whenever the opportunities arose. My first instrument was actually the piano, or at least it was the family piano that resided in the living room, but which had been bought specifically for me to practise on. It was a family tradition in both my mum's and dad's families that there was a piano in the house and the kids all took lessons. I struggled with it for a couple of years, and learned some useful basics, but never really took to it.

The bongos were a surprise holiday gift one year from my grandparents - only a cheap pair sold to tourists in Acapulco - but the gift was really a life-changing moment for me. I absolutely loved them - everything about them - not just the sounds, but the look, the feel and the smell of them. So that really fired my interest in drums and percussion, and I got my first drum kit a few years later.

I taught myself to play drums, as well as some basic guitar, but all within the confines of the teenage bedroom. I went away to college when I was 18 and hardly played anything until after graduating. I still loved music - I was buying loads of records, going to gigs, helping out with gigs and discos at college, and so on. But I wasn't playing, and never really thought about it.

It was a couple of years after leaving college, when my girlfriend and I got our first flat in East London, that I replied to an advert in a newsagent window and joined my first band - a soul and blues band playing the pub circuit on and around the Isle of Dogs. We rehearsed a couple of times a week and played for beer.

The opportunity to join Dead Can Dance came about by pure chance. As I mentioned earlier, Brendan, Lisa and original bassist Paul Erikson, came to London from Australia in 1982 in search of a record deal, but their original drummer couldn't make the trip. They ended up in a flat close to where I lived, put word out they were looking for a drummer, that word reached me and as they couldn't even afford to place a small ad in the NME at the time, they had no option but to give me the drum stool. Within six months we had a deal with 4AD, and suddenly I was 'a musician'!

On tour, Brendan had a literally hair-raising experience. That was our first ever gig abroad, when 4AD put us onto an 8-date tour of Holland with the Cocteau Twins in late 1983. The first date was at the Paradiso in Amsterdam and when we were called to do our soundcheck, we discovered (in glorious naivety) that nobody had realised that they have different electrical plugs in Europe. All our equipment was fitted with UK 3-pin plugs, so someone had to run out and get a load of European 2-pins which then had to be fitted in a mad rush. The soundcheck went OK, but once the show started, we were about four songs into our set when there was suddenly a huge 'bang', big flash of blue light and Brendan appeared to jump about three feet into the air. The audience thought it was some cool pyrotechnic effect and applauded, and at first Scott (then bassist) and I continued playing (having been drilled by Brendan NEVER to stop in the middle of a song) and not realising at that point what was happening. Brendan started shaking alarmingly and Lisa ran to help him. Luckily the on-stage sound engineer realised immediately that Brendan's guitar had gone live and was now stuck to his body with the full mains current surging through him and earthing into the stage. He ran over, pushed Lisa back (had she grabbed Brendan, she would have been sucked into the circuit) and managed to spectacularly kung-fu kick Brendan's guitar off him. Brendan staggered off stage, severely shaken. It was only afterwards that we discovered that the replacement plug had been wired incorrectly, resulting in Brendan nearly being killed.

My involvement with DCD is 100% positive - there are no negatives. I had amazing experiences recording and touring Europe and America with DCD. And then subsequently I have had my solo 'career' which simply would never have been possible had it not been for DCD and, in particular, Brendan. It was Brendan's suggestion in 1995 that I should make a solo album, and he put his studio and his own time at my disposal. He had a huge input into my 'Pathways and Dawns' album - engineering, arranging, playing parts and producing six of the eight tracks. Without him, it would just not have happened.

When I came to make *Enter The Mysterium* a few years later, I felt I needed to do it without Brendan's input to prove to myself that I could - though, of course, I found myself constantly referring back in my mind to things he had taught me, or things I had picked up from watching him work.

This sequence of events made the progression of my albums unusual in that my second album is more raw and earthy in feel than the first which is more 'polished'. Usually it goes the other way but, although I remain very happy with both albums, in some ways I feel more comfortable with the rugged qualities of *Mysterium*, and it's satisfying to know I did that (albeit with the valuable input of engineer/co-producer Hill Briggs).

I think most reviewers tend to be aware of my past connections with Dead Can Dance, whose music certainly does possess a spiritual dimension, so when I put out an album of songs – *Enter The Mysterium* - exploring various mysteries and beliefs, many reviewers naturally made the assumption that I was attempting to write spiritual music. But this is not the case. If people want to listen and enjoy the music as it is, or want to read and interpret the words in their own way, I am very happy about that. But for anyone who wants to read the explanation behind each song, my website at www.TheMysterium.info will reveal all. And it will also demonstrate that my role is one of 'observer'. I am not a spiritual person writing from spiritual experience. But I am passionately interested in my subject matters, and I hope that I therefore treat them with the sensitivity and impartiality that I strive for.

The background to *Enter The Mysterium* is this. Sometime in 2001, I went to a concert at the South Bank Centre in London by Joglaresa, an intriguing early music group led by Belinda Sykes who is both a musician/singer and a professor of medieval song and authority on Arabic music. The concert was of music recreated from the time of the Crusades, and the programme notes included mention of a phenomenon I had never previously heard of - 'the True Cross'. I subsequently researched this further and discovered a very colourful history surrounding the travels and ultimate fate of this wooden artefact, believed to have been the central section cut from the cross on which Jesus was crucified and which came to be a potent symbol of the conflict between Christians and Muslims in the wars over control of the Holy Lands.

I felt moved to write my own song specifically about The True Cross and musically reflecting the historic setting, and this became the first song written for my follow-up album to *Pathways and Dawns*. Having completed it and started to think about song number two, the idea occurred to me to write an album of songs about different mysteries and beliefs, with each subject inspiring a different musical setting. I set about researching potential song subjects and became thoroughly absorbed in the whole process.

In the summer of 2002, when I was about half way through writing the album, I was browsing in a bookshop for a couple of paperbacks to take on holiday and by chance came across The Queen's Conjuror by Benjamin Woolley and instinctively bought it, mainly because I liked the cover. It turned out to be a biography of a 16th century doctor called John Dee who was simultaneously a member of the court of Queen Elizabeth I of England, by virtue of his position of physician to the Queen, whilst being widely treated as an outcast and held in deep mistrust because of his dabblings in alchemy, clandestine experiments and his obsessive pursuit of answers to the great universal mysteries through meetings with angels. As part of his quest for knowledge, Dee accumulated an extraordinary library of ancient and contemporary texts at his house in Mortlake, creating one of the finest libraries of its time outside the major religious and academic institutions.

Up to my discovery of the Dee book, I had felt slightly uncomfortable that the album I was writing was a little too disjointed and needed some kind of central thread to pull together the disparate parts. By making the album an allegorical visit to a latter-day Dee's library, where the visitor can dip at random into any tome plucked from the shelf and enter the world of some mystery or belief, I felt I had a more cohesive form.

I then wrote the album's opening song – *At Mortlake* - to set the scene, and its second song – *The Scryer and the Shewstone* to specifically explore an aspect of Dee's life, following which the songs appear in the order in which I felt the album best flowed musically, but always (in my mind) staying in the context of the library of discovery.

The title I then chose for the album – *Enter The Mysterium* - came partly from a series of books which Dee wrote called the *Liber Mysteriorum* (Books of Mysteries) and partly to convey the idea of entering an 'emporium of mysteries'.

Having completed the album and given it its context, however, I was acutely aware that I did not want to overstate the importance of the research behind the album and potentially distance the music from anyone not interested in that aspect. Thus, the CD cover booklet merely reproduces the lyrics and says nothing of the context. But, as I said previously, for anyone who wants to read the explanation behind each song, my website at www.TheMysterium.info will reveal all.

I look to many different areas for sources of inspiration for songs. There were a couple of personal songs on my first solo album, *Pathways and Dawns* - for example *Life Amongst The Black Sheep* is about my early years of parenthood and *The Springs of Hope* mirrors my generally optimistic outlook on life - but for the most part I find it difficult to write directly from personal experience. I dislike the blandness, cliches and superficiality of the bulk of modern lyricism. I have great admiration for songwriters like Jarvis Cocker and Guy Garvey who write wonderfully incisive, witty and emotional takes on the loves and lives of the ordinary man - I can appreciate that, but I can't do it. Similarly, I love the strange and abstract world of Thom Yorke. But, I'm too pragmatic to be comfortable writing in that kind of territory, so I have to look for areas where I do feel comfortable.

I've had pretty much a life-long interest in other cultures - the more different the life to mine, the more it fascinates me. These could be other contemporary cultures in locations far from where I lived most of my life in the metropolis of London, or they could be historic. I've always been attracted to magazine articles, books, TV documentaries, etc on such subjects - as well as to exploring the music of all 'alien' cultures.

I'm motivated and inspired by just simply any music that moves me. I think that's probably the same for most people who do anything creative. When you hear film-makers interviewed, it seems to me they nearly always recount childhood experiences of going to the cinema and being enthralled and deciding "I want to do that". I've always had that kind of response to music - when I hear something I love, it can often make me feel like going and writing something.

I think you also have to feel that you have something to offer, that in approaching creativity you don't just set out to imitate what has inspired you, but you are motivated because you can see a different angle, a different direction in which to take an idea and thus craft it into something of your own.

I do find myself very drawn to atmospheres in music - I like to be enveloped by the sound of a piece rather than just tickled by a pretty tune. So, when I write, I am also trying to paint pictures and create moods. Before I met Brendan, I had no idea how to achieve that - and he is still the master - but from him I picked up the basics that I now use and which, hopefully, I will continue to develop.

I have this massive attraction to musical instruments. It's everything about them - look, sound(s), feel, smell - only the sense of taste misses out. There is a magic about an instrument - every instrument is so full of possibilities, the starting point to a beautiful melody or a rousing rhythm. I also find it really interesting to know about the culture from which an instrument originates.

I feel a bit of a fraud with that instrument list for *Enter the Mysterium*. I do genuinely play a lot of different instruments on the album, but mostly only very simple parts. I'm not trying to fool anyone into thinking that I'm an amazing multi-instrumentalist, because I really am not. But if you go into the studio with an armoury of different instruments, you can always find something to add a different colouration or texture, maybe just with a couple of notes. But then I think it's interesting to tell people what all those different sounds are.

In *The Scryer and the Shewstone*, there is a part which should be played on a renaissance wind instrument - probably something like a serpent or (more likely) a crumhorn. But I don't have one and don't know anyone who does, so I improvised and mimicked the part by humming into a kazoo (remember them? - like a posh version of putting a bit of tracing paper over a comb). The studio engineer added some effects to the sound and we thought we'd done a damn fine job of disguising it. The first person I played the demo to - an old compatriate from my Isle of Dogs pub band - immediately said "Blimey, I 'aven't 'eard a kazoo for years!" Can't win 'em all.

I am happy that I am, all the time, developing my own audience and that my Venn diagram has a growing area beyond the overlap with DCD. My current label - City Canyons Records in New York - is playing a vital role in this as they have no historic connection with anything DCD-related or any artists working in 'Goth', 'darkwave', 'ethereal' or any of the genres with which DCD has been associated. Having said all that, DCD will always be a big presence in what I do and where I have come from, and I will always embrace that.

Having made the albums, I needed to find a label to release them and, once again, without having the DCD association, I am not sure I would have been able to interest anybody - it would certainly have been a lot harder. Dropping the DCD name, particularly in the US where DCD is very big, opened a lot of doors.

It was a very deliberate move on my part to approach City Canyons with regards to the release of *Mysterium* as it was, at the time, a small but highly energetic and ambitious label looking to build a very diverse roster of artists and going for mainstream audiences. I thought if I could interest them in my music, it would be very interesting to see where this could lead. Luckily, label head Trebor Lloyd loved the demo I sent in (his favourite song is track 9, so he must really have listened all through it!!) and we quickly agreed terms. I became only the third artist signed to the label, so I was there from early days. Trebor has boundless energy and enthusiasm, a very wide ranging taste, and also a background in theatre. He also had creative ambitions, as I was to discover. The City Canyons website can be found at www.citycanyons.com

My logo was originally Trebor's idea. When we started working on ideas for the cover of *Enter The Mysterium*, he asked me if I'd ever thought about using a symbol image. I hadn't, but I liked the idea. I already had it firmly fixed in my mind that I wanted to use the two door pictures on the front and back covers, but the idea of a symbol for use on the actual disc and perhaps elsewhere in the cover booklet appealed to me.

I started looking through books of symbols, but everything I found already had too many other associations, and I wanted something different. The only answer was to create my own image.

I took a series of well-known symbols - the all-seeing eye, the sun, the Cardinal points, the serpent, rune signs for fire and water, the Islamic crescent moon, the Christian cross, etc, and combined them into my own image which contains at least one symbol relevant to each song on the album.

When I sent it to Trebor, he loved it and so we decided to use it extensively as an image to represent both me as artist and the album.

I like the way City Canyons' designer, R K Watkins, used it as a recurring image through the cover booklet and disc.

In a funny way, the image later reminded me of a symbol/logo which my old favourite 70s band Nektar used on their early album covers which combined a bee, cut-away body (part human, part insect), and skeleton guitar - quite different imagery, but the compository format and overall shape bear similarities. Perhaps another subliminal influence?

Again, once the albums were released and we went out into the market seeking exposure/reviews/airplay etc, the DCD connection would come into play, gaining me a lot more coverage in the US than had I been the solo artist from nowhere.

The one danger was that my music would be compared too directly with DCD and my voice with Brendan's, in which circumstances I would, of course, always be found wanting.

However, I've found that most reviewers have always taken a very considerate stance on this, realising that I am not putting myself forward as any kind of extension of, or alternative to DCD, but rather that I have created my own sound with DCD as an important reference point.

When I look back through my press cuttings file, I am surprised and touched by so many glowing reviews, and I have to say there is a genuine warmth and desire to like what I do from people who have clearly been moved so deeply by DCD in the past.

This is also reflected very strongly in comments from people who have contacted me online and who understand and appreciate what I am doing with a depth and passion that never ceases to move me. It is truly wonderful to have this connection with people all over the world through my music.

The big problem in promoting my music, particularly here in the UK, has always been that I don't fit anywhere. It's all very well being 'eclectic', but from a marketing point of view, it can be quite disastrous not to fit neatly into a pigeon-hole. It means that when you send an unsolicited review CD to the mainstream media, the person receiving it either sends it to the rock, or jazz, or folk critic - any of whom will take a quick listen and say "that's not my area" - or thinks "I haven't got a clue who to send this to for review". Either way, the review copy ends up in the bin or down the local charity shop and no review appears. Same situation with radio stations, and hence radio airplay has largely eluded me.

One of Peter's songs, '*The Scryer and the Shewstone*', is on the John Barleycorn Reborn album which won an 'Innovation Of The Year' award from the Fatea Folk Magazine. I asked Peter to tell me about it.

A friend of mine - Steve Tyler of the wonderful early music group Misericordia - tipped me off that Mark Coyle who was running the Woven Wheat Whispers download site was compiling an album of dark British folk music. I contacted Mark, who was very welcoming to my approach, sent him a copy of *Mysterium*, and he came back to me really eager to include a track on his *John Barleycorn Reborn* compilation.

The album was released a few months later and I was really pleased to have been involved. It's a brilliant compilation of very varied music from a wildly varied set of bands/artists, most of whom are/were little known and would have been struggling to achieve exposure in the same way I was. But as a collective whole, the JBR album has took on a life force of its own and made a big impression.

The album received a glowing review in Songlines magazine (their 50th anniversary issue) and another great review in Choice, a free magazine put out through all branches of HMV, which also gave the album prime rack positions in its chain of stores. Additionally, JBR won the FATEA award which you mention, and was featured on Stuart Maconie's 'Freakzone' show on BBC Radio 6, with my song being one of the two tracks chosen for airplay. These were major breakthroughs as far as I was concerned - a level of exposure I'd never been able to achieve on my own.

As for the song itself, I left the selection to Mark Coyle. Initially he planned to use *The Witchbottle of Suffolk* from *Mysterium* - which is the 'darkest' song on my album, but at the last minute he changed his mind and selected *The Scryer and the Shewstone* which recounts some of Dr John Dee's recorded meetings with angels through his scryer (medium) Edward Kelley.

The JBR album was, in itself, a major research project by Mark and is supported by a fascinating website full of dark folklore, antiquated anecdotes and great imagery, which can be found at www.john-barleycorn-reborn.com

Shortly after I did the first interview for *Mind & Motivation* a completely unforeseen change of direction took place. I had been giving some thought to a starting point for material for my third solo album when Trebor asked me if I'd be interested in working on a collaborative track – something for which he had written lyrics and for which he would like to use a female vocalist he was working with in New York at the time, but with me initially writing and arranging the music. I'd never worked from this kind of angle before so jumped at the opportunity, and he sent me his words for *Hanging Man* and gave me carte blanche for the score.

The lyrics are dark, and the setting has connotations of an

early settler community in the Appalachian Mountains, so I did my best to reflect that in my initial writing and arrangement. I also felt a Celtic element fitted the piece, so included an instrumental bridge for Uilleann pipes and Irish whistle which were performed by a friend of my younger daughter. I sent it off to Trebor, who seemed happy with it and set to work on his side of the Atlantic. A few weeks later I received back an arrangement with his own musical developments and topped with the wonderful voice of Sara Wendt, an established artist on the New York scene who Trebor had recently signed to City Canyons. We were all delighted with the result, and it was a real thrill to have been involved in a creative process with so many more dimensions than working in my own isolation.

I then invited an artist/photographer friend, Tony Pinfold, to make a phased slide video which we uploaded to YouTube with some great imagery, and there could be little doubt that we had the start of a project worthy of pursuit. "The Peter Ulrich Collaboration" was born, with the intention to retain the freedom to involve whoever we chose, but with me being the omnipresent performer and Trebor the director and producer.

At this point I would say there was no specific vision for how the project would develop, but Trebor immediately expanded the core group of contributors, bringing in UK vocalist David Steele (another recent signing to City Canyons) and a long-time friend and colleague from the New York scene, Anne Husick, who became one of the three core writers alongside Trebor and me.

I seem to recall it was once we had three completed songs under our collective belt that we took the decision that we would work towards a full album's-worth of material. Much in the same vein as I had previously approached my solo albums, each song featured a different mix of instruments and took an entirely different rhythmic/compositional approach. I discovered that Trebor had an impressively vast range of contacts in the New York scene and we ended up with 12 songs featuring some 40 musicians and probably not far short of double that number of instruments … we really indulged ourselves!

Working with Trebor also had a very good dynamic – he forced the pace and, while I have a tendency after I've completed an album to sit back and wait to see what happens with that release before considering my next move, 'TPUC' under Trebor's impetus just kept writing and recording. The first TPUC album, *The Painted Caravan*, was released in 2013 and the second, *Tempus Fugitives*, in 2015 – somewhat different to the six year gap between my solo releases!

The project gathered some great reviews – the respected higherplainmusic.com website announced "The Painted Caravan is utterly phenomenal from start to finish… Easily a contender for album of the year", while mainstream highbrow UK newspaper The Financial Times (no less!) described our same debut album as "an insane throwback of a record, thrumming with bagpipes, mariachi brass, hammered dulcimer, Chinese guitar, a flutter of flutes and plainchant".

Tempus Fugitives saw us extend our list of participants (and instruments) even further, with what emerged as one of the most popular tracks – *Dark Daddy* - featuring the beautiful voice and harp-playing of Erin Hill. The album release was swiftly followed by the one TPUC live performance to date in June 2015 in New York. This was really Trebor's "piece de resistance" and I am eternally grateful to him for what was a truly amazing experience.

He managed to get us a booking in Webster Hall, a famous old venue in Lower East Side which I understand to have been played by luminaries including Sinatra and Clapton, and reputedly the location of Bob Dylan's first recorded TV appearance in 1962. He also put together an extraordinary 17-piece band, including Erin's husband Mike Nolan as on-stage musical director (combined with masterful pedal steel guitar playing), and co-ordinated a mind-bogglingly complex rehearsal schedule given the wildly varying commitments of the participants. I flew out to New York a few weeks before the date to join up with the rest of the band and managed to slot in fairly seamlessly, thanks to the professionalism and great camaraderie of the ensemble. And, by all reports, we put on a damn fine show.

It had already been pretty much decided by this stage that TPUC would make a trilogy of albums as it has been too big a project to commit to indefinitely. We now have the third album "in the can" awaiting its release schedule, so the imminent future will be the promotion of *Final Reflections* and then deciding what next… watch this space…

Chapter 5
Innovation

Innovation is the ability to progress ideas and come to fresh insights, to perceive new possibilities that can arise from old structures. It creates the emergence of a new paradigm, where the previous state acts as a springboard to the conception of a broader framework. This moves us further along our evolutionary path, while affecting both our inner perceptions and our outward expression of them. The word 'innovate' is derived from the Latin 'innovat – innovare,' which means 'to renew, to alter.' This implies a step forward that does not totally reject what has gone before, but incorporates it into the new, adds an extra dimension, and leads to fresh discoveries.

Without the quality of innovation, our species would have remained caught in the distant past, trapped in the harsh world of the Stone Age. We would still be living in caves, at the mercy of the weather and the success or failure of the hunt, choosing our leaders for their physical strength and their ability to keep the tribe alive and together. At an instinctive level, very little has changed over the millennia. We still live by these ancient, instinctual codes, despite our modern technological sophistication. We elect leaders with the aim of keeping the tribe strong, although nowadays we hope that their leadership qualities will be gained through wisdom rather than brute force. Instead of hunting with shards of rock, slings or spears, we do our daily work in order to bring home currency that can be exchanged for comfortable shelter from the elements, and for food and warmth. Yet our distant ancestors, if they were transported to our time, would consider us to be gods – and would view us as the great beings who were reputed to have left their imprint on past civilisations. Our worldview, and our ability to control forces such as electricity, would be awe-inspiring. So, where in our culture has innovation helped us to evolve? How have we arrived from there, to here?

THE EUREKA! EFFECT

The new evolutionary eras created through the taming of fire and the invention of the wheel allowed our progression towards more technological capabilities. Someone, back in the recesses of our tribal past, watched, noticed, made a mental connection, and Eureka! changed the perception and evolution of the entire tribe and its subsequent generations. Through these discoveries life gradually became less arduous, which allowed more time for contemplation and gave rise to yet more ideas. The dreams of the cave dweller gazing into the fire at the end of the day expanded through the ages, became more complex. Like the creation of a necklace, each new idea, concept and discovery added another bead to the basic string that had been manifest since the first human being. The process of evolution through innovation is a holoistic progression, an unfolding through a seemingly convoluted terrain that rippled backwards and forwards as cultures rose, fell, and rose again.

A HOLOISTIC VIEW

A holon is a term described by Arthur Koestler which indicates an entity that is whole within itself yet is also part of a larger entity. The cells within our body are individual microscopic universes, yet they also exist as part of the organism that is our body. The consciousness of the cell is included within the consciousness of the body. Each of us, as a holon, contains within our DNA every possible factor that makes up human nature.

Our DNA is the blueprint for our species, containing within its beaded strands all of the codes that can be accessed, every possibility for the blossoming of potential. We all express individual aspects, but we are all also connected at a fundamental intra-cellular and sub-cellular level. We are all part of the complex necklace of life. The concept of the holon is effective from the most subtle quantum states (an atom is part of a molecule, a molecule is part of a cell) and expands through to the perception of the entire cosmos as being the container of each individual part of itself. Life is expressed holoistically. Each entity is complete within itself, yet also exists as a fraction of something greater.

In the context of evolution and innovation, the new encompasses what has gone before. It incorporates it, extends it, expands it, and leads it into a further dimension in an unfolding process that is ongoing. The holon that is yourself encompasses the holon that was your Stone Age ancestor, your medieval ancestor, your Victorian ancestor. They live within us as part of our past, and also of our future. We step up on their shoulders, climb up the next rung of the ladder, but we never fully leave them behind, as the ladder could not retain its structure without the rungs that hold it together from below.

In our society, we have more opportunity than ever before in which to think, to ponder, to experiment. Despite the current pressure to fill every waking moment with activity, less hours in our daily life need to be taken up with survival issues. We have more leisure to dream, and more available instruments that can aid our dreaming. In that dreaming lies the seeds of our future. The danger to ourselves and our planet arises when we become arrogant and forget our holoistic nature; when we think that we are autonomous, that we are the gods that our ancestors would perceive us to be. If the cells in our body were to think that they did not need the body – if they perceived themselves as whole, but not part of a larger organism – they would become pathological, and the body, the whole organism, would die. This is what happens in diseases such as cancer. The holoistic image of the body is lost, sacrificed to the departure of a single cell from what is healthy and natural. If we forget or ignore our holoistic nature, forget that we are cells in the body of a larger whole; forget to dream, to vision, to imagine, then we become caught up in negative imagery, succumb to a pathological condition and destroy not only ourselves, but also the larger organisms that we are part of – our families, our culture, our ecosystem, our planet. The dream becomes a nightmare that leads to annihilation.

THE VITALITY OF REFLECTION

Our ancestors knew this. The survival and safety of the tribe depended upon the integrity and interrelationship of each of its members. We hold that memory within us, deep within the core of the instinctual self, and forget it or ignore it at our peril. Our ancestors' opportunities for leisure came through gazing into the fire or up at the stars; through painting their magical images on cave walls and inscribing them into stones and the Earth herself. Over the ages, the gradual developments of discoveries emerging through trial and error, sudden insights or serendipity have freed up humanity to mine richer veins within its own mind. And like a muscle, the more the mind is used, the more effectively it gives of its secrets; our filters thin out to allow through an increased traffic of information. The magnified ability to reflect, and to develop ourselves through these reflections, has led us up the spiral ladder one rung at a time from the foundations laid in humanity's distant past.

THE SEARCH FOR ESSENCE

Yet the evolution of our species has taken place on more than the material level. Innovation is the discovery of new ways of thinking and being, and without these the external developments would be worthless except as toys and playthings. The fundamental change has been in our perception of the roots of our spiritual nature; our relationship with the All That Is, the spiritual essence. Early humankind *externalised* that energy, that force. It was seen as being in the moon, the sun, the stars, the elements, but not within themselves. A mediator was needed in the form of a shaman, priest or priestess to act as interpreter. Propitiation of the gods was costly in terms of time and often of life (both human and animal), and the power to control the tribe's spiritual and secular development lay in the hands of the mediators.

Through the succeeding millennia, sages and teachers have emerged whose knowledge has been disseminated cross-culturally, and this is now being wedded with the discoveries of the new sciences. The external perception of the All That Is, the sought-after state of unity, completion, fulfilment is now being *internalised.* Awareness is growing that this rests within us as a natural state, that we can all be mediators and communicators with the Whole, because we are all part of the whole. That whether or not we choose to understand and express our connection with the Ultimate makes no difference whatsoever to its existence.

AS WITHOUT, SO WITHIN

This has been the basis of all emerging forms of mysticism and is now being discovered through quantum cosmology. The building blocks of creation hum within every cell of our body. The universe(s) exist as a wave function. The eminent physicist, Professor Stephen Hawking, replaced the word 'particle' with the word 'universe.' We live within a wave of probability, wherein all is possible. And the great gift, the great innovation of our era, lies in the recognition of this, along with the realisation that essence comes from within and radiates to without, and not the other way around. Our spirituality, our life-force, our connection with the Whole rests within us. Our definition of our lives, our universe, and our relationship with the All is continually created anew through our perception of it in each and every moment.

It has always been so. The old saying that there is nothing new under the sun is true. And yet we continually undergo a process of re-discovery, re-cognition, and this leads us on a dance that moves us further along the spiral, circling onwards and upwards, as we stand on the shoulders of our parents, and our children stand on our shoulders, and so on. The spiral ladder reaches further than we can ever see as we gaze upwards from the rung we stand on; up into dizzying heights that are beyond our comprehension.

The soil beneath the ladder has always been there – the fertile mind-stuff that cradles in its depths the embryonic seeds of ideas, visions and all possibilities. It seems that Mind existed long before our bodies, before the body of the cosmos, before time itself. And our evolution from the first cave dwellers to the here and now has been the process of germination, of sprouting, of the development of those seeds that initially needed outer gods to give them direction and purpose. At that time humankind was not ready, or able, to realise that within the seed lies the blueprint, the entelechy, the fractal image, the imprint of holism. Now, at our current stage of development we are able to glimpse this, to stretch out tendrils within our minds to encompass and embrace the glowing flame that exists within us; to allow ignition to take place.

THE PEARL IN THE OYSTER

The keys to innovation are openness and curiosity. What gives rise to innovation is the inner itch that must be scratched, dealt with. It comes most often when we feel cornered, boxed in, when we are searching for a solution, knowing that there is something there, waiting for a connection to be made. It is the *question* that will not go away until an answer is found. Just as a pearl is created through the lodging of a piece of grit within an oyster, the *irritation*, the itch experienced by the oyster generates something new, beautiful and precious. The pearl has aptly been viewed as the symbol of wisdom. Irritation is the impulse for change, the spur that gives rise to life. The inner itch that sets innovative thinking in motion stems from the realisation that something is no longer working, does not fit together, that a fresh viewpoint is needed. We scratch this itch by asking "What? Why? How?" which then leads us into "What if….?" And a new possibility can then be born within us. We are all wisdom-keepers. We all contain a pearl within us. We all, at some point in our lives, feel the sharp bite of grit lodging in our inner being, though the circumstances that lead to the perception of its itching, its discomfort, its irritation are different for everyone. During our lives, most of us experience at some time the chasm, the vortex that threatens to swallow us in its dark maw. We have all struggled in its grip, striven to break free of it, break away, deny, escape; we have refused to ask the question that insists on an answer. And we have finally realised that the only way through is down, down, into the murky silt that lines the bed of our deepest fears. Like pearl divers we take a breath and plunge, not knowing what treasures our fingers will grasp.

What we emerge with, gasping and bruised but elated, is the answer we have sought, the pearl that has grown through the itch, through the discomfort. We have created a thing of beauty, a jewel, through the quest for an answer. Innovation arises when the status quo cannot remain static any longer, when there is no way back and the way forward is unclear. We are forced into an internal quantum shift that has wide external repercussions. We change. We grow. We recognise our inherent creative nature. And new ideas, new worlds are born.

Curiosity is the parent of knowledge. And we are essentially curious beings, blessed with questing minds. Even in less gritty phases of our lives, when the most important questions rest beneath the surface and refrain from poking and prodding us, the human mind perpetually seeks the new even while it enjoys the comfort of the old tried and tested paradigms. This is fundamental to our nature.

Children want to know *everything*. As soon as they begin to talk, a barrage of questions tumbles from their lips. "How? What? Who? Where? Why, why, why? What if….?" If their questions are answered, brief illumination shines from their faces, followed swiftly by more questions. The world to a young child is a fascinating, mysterious place, and every moment is an adventure just waiting to be embarked upon, explored, understood. Every moment holds a wealth of possibilities, and each of these contain the promise of being a key to the child's understanding of his or her place in the scheme of things. The reason most children resist bedtime is because they simply cannot bear to miss anything.

We do not have to leave this curiosity behind when we reach adulthood. It is necessary throughout life. The most interesting companions are those who are fascinated by everything and everyone they come into contact with. Their 'child-like' need to *know* makes them very appealing, because they generate an infectious sense of excitement, of delight in life and all it holds in store. Our openness, our sense of being awake and aware within each moment, generates an enquiring attitude, helps us to see doorways into the new, keeps us asking questions and finding answers. This enhances our receptivity, creativity, and innovative thinking. It helps us to bring the seemingly unlikely into the realms of the possible. An open attitude enables the ability to view apparently diverse elements and to make connections between them; to experience mental leaps that lead to a fusion of previously unrelated constituents to create a fresh perspective, a heady brew of insights. The greatest philosophers, scientists, artists, writers, investigators and inventors have all possessed this quality in abundance.

LEFT BRAIN, RIGHT BRAIN

The process of new ideas and principles that lead to innovation employ both the left and right hemispheres of the brain. Without this synthesis, ideas could not be put to practical application. Our purpose in discovering who we are and why we are here needs to be expressed as well as realised. The urge to recognise and experience wholeness within ourselves is accelerated when we can follow through on intuitive insights by putting them to practical use.

Our brains are divided into two distinct hemispheres, and each 'side' has specific functions and controls the opposite side of the body. The left hemisphere governs the right side of the body, while the right hemisphere controls the left side of the body. The left brain is concerned with logical processes, reasoning, analysis, and rational thinking. The right brain governs artistic abilities, spatial processes, creativity and intuition. A focus on developing the left hemisphere gives rise to areas of work and interest that involve *serial* processes – logical steps taken one after another, in progression. Statisticians, mathematicians, scientists, computer programmers make predominant use of the left hemisphere of the brain. The right brain enables *parallel* processes to occur, giving the ability to see a wide perspective, to visualise, to follow through on feelings and intuitions. Artists, musicians, philosophers, visionaries make more use of the right hemisphere of the brain. In brief, the left brain rules linear thinking, while the right brain rules lateral thinking.

The focus within our society has been primarily geared towards left brain, linear processes, and our education system reflects this in its attitude towards learning. Yet both hemispheres are equally important. Scientists experience flashes of insight that are right-brained, and then follow these through with logical, serial processes in order to develop a new theory and give credence to it. A musician accesses the right brain, yet also needs to use the left-brained serial processes in order to write or follow a musical score. This book, like most books, began with a sudden idea, complete within itself, but was followed by the serial processes of putting the ideas into a logical, understandable order, and the undertaking of research to check facts. Recently a new theory has emerged that a third brain exists, a central area that deals with the perception of unity and the spiritual aspect of the self. If proven, this could be the bedrock as well as the connecting area between the left and right hemispheres.

What gives maximum potency to the revelatory insights that lead to innovation is the application of those insights for our own benefit and that of others. The conscious employment of both hemispheres of the brain enables us to access all of the areas within ourselves. If you are primarily intuitive, more accustomed to using the right brain, you can strengthen the connection with the left brain through taking up a form of study that requires a more linear perspective, or by using a computer for setting down creative ideas. If you are primarily logical, using the left brain more, you can deepen the access to the right brain through music, or poetry, or philosophical works, or painting, or studying intuitive areas of healing or divination. When we perceive both aspects of ourselves as being able to work together in harmony, we feel more 'whole' within ourselves, and more open-minded. This enables us to perceive a richer sense of purpose in our lives.

INDEPENDENT THINKING

To make discoveries, to be innovative, to open ourselves to possibilities, we need to be able to stand alone. If we are constantly seeking approval or approbation from others, (which is what most of us are taught to do as children) this can block the free flow of ideas and associations, along with our sense of discovery and self-expression. Evolution is impossible without innovation, and innovation cannot occur without the facility and the impulse to follow through on the flashes of insights that are generated.

In our culture we are encouraged to view ourselves through the eyes of others, which means being subjected to (sometimes overruled by) others' opinions of us. Because of this, our self-perception is often based on a distorted mirror image rather than reality. If we are constantly told we are this, or that, it can colour our own opinions of ourselves, and this deflects our attention from who *we* perceive ourselves to be. This mirroring of others can be helpful if we use it to see qualities in other people and recognise them in ourselves, because it reduces the potential for judgmental attitudes. What do we see when we gaze into the eyes of another person? We see an image of ourselves reflected back. We all act as reflections, and the primary purpose of this is to help us to recognise that within each of us is contained (in varying proportions) every quality and characteristic that makes up human nature in its totality. We are holons. Our individuality arises through our expression of what comes most naturally to us, and our purpose rests within that expression.

The ability to step out of the conventional, traditional mind-set, to follow your individuality, is crucial to the emergence of new ideas. This demands courage and confidence, as an innovative approach is often initially met with opposition. On rare occasions a new concept will spark a positive reaction in the mass consciousness because it comes at a critical point when many people are open, ready and waiting for change. A chord is struck that resonates in many minds simultaneously, a shift takes place, and a new paradigm comes into being.

CREATING NEW STRUCTURE

More commonly, it takes time for new ideas to be accepted. The nature of a paradigm is structure, and that structure includes boundaries that can be difficult to surmount without a strong impetus of energy and the direct application of willpower. The communication of insights that break down the old paradigm are often greeted at first with disbelief, then ridicule, then finally acceptance. If the inner truth that you are expressing does not coincide with the perspective of others, you need tenacity and determination in order to hold on to your belief in yourself and persuade others to listen to you.

Over the last century we have witnessed a vast expansion of technical and scientific innovations. Our great-grandparents and grandparents have experienced the emergence of cars, electricity, aeroplanes, washing machines, microwave ovens, television, space travel, cardiac pacemakers, organ transplants, computers, the internet, mobile phones – just to mention a few of the recent developments. We have grown accustomed to communicating via the telephone and internet. We shudder collectively at the rise of sophisticated weaponry that could annihilate virtually all life on our planet. We view the increasing possibilities of artificial intelligence. We have been opened up to ideas in theoretical physics and cosmology that are providing a new framework for our knowledge about the universe. We are realising that Uni-verse translates as 'one song', and we are now able to begin to pick out some of the notes that provide the underlying framework for the melody. Every year more discoveries are made, and this is accelerating.

META-PHYSICS

And this is merely the external aspect! Major shifts have also come about in the perception of consciousness. We have observed the transplantation of Eastern philosophies and have begun to merge these with the Western spiritual paradigm. Science, viewed since the time of Newton as being separate from God, is now experiencing an about-turn, providing philosophical and spiritual implications that challenge the mind into a direct confrontation with issues around the nature of consciousness. Machines can now photograph the aura, the subtle energy field around life-forms, revealing that we are far more than merely a material body. The vision of Earth photographed from space generated the realisation that we inhabit a global village, and that 'home' implies far more than merely the house or the country we live in. The images generated by the Hubble telescope remind us that we are an infinitely small speck in our own galaxy, and that the Milky Way is merely a fleck among the countless other galaxies embroidered into the fabric of space. And meanwhile, the new theories in physics reveal to us that we are all created from the same, immeasurably small, stuff of life, and so are kin to everything in existence.

At the same time, we are learning to explore our inner space through the upsurge of interest in counselling, hypnotherapy, psychology, complementary therapies and meditation. Systems that are developed with the purpose of enhancing self-knowledge are now commonplace and are being used to great effect in large companies and conglomerates as well as in individual homes. And the more we discover about ourselves, the more we perceive the interrelationship and interconnections between ourselves and others. The concept of 'us and them' becomes invalid when we see ourselves reflected in each other's eyes.

Our personal discovery of our inner purpose is amplified by our internal resonance with the rest of our species, with other species of creatures that share this planet, and with the cosmos as a whole. Each new insight that creates a shift within us, through our ability to embrace and express the innovative aspects of ourselves, brings about a shift in the consciousness of the whole. The Greek philosopher Plato spoke of the realm of ideas as thought-forms. Our experiences of, and feelings about, life are connected to the thoughts which we bring into form. When we expand our consciousness, we realise that we each encompass the whole. We live in a holographic uni-verse, and the ideas that create new paradigms are accessible to all of us, if we allow our curiosity free rein and open ourselves to what is within and around us.

Reminder: Your ability to remain open to all possibilities creates expansion that encompasses all areas of your life.

Question to ponder: What facilitates a state within you of making connections between ideas?

EXERCISES

Exercise 1. Perception and feeling

Pay attention to your changes of mood and note in your journal how your perception shifts depending upon how you are feeling. When do you experience a sense of connection, however fleeting?
Take a daily routine such as preparing a meal. Notice your attitude and feelings during this.
If you are in a hurry, or distracted, does this become a chore?
If you are relaxed, can you absorb yourself in the process of self-nourishment?
Observing how your perceptions are governed by your mood helps you to be more in control of your life.

Exercise 2. Evaluation

As a child, you questioned everything. Have you maintained that intense curiosity? In your journal, divide a page into 4 sections, headed Emotional Life, Work Life, Play, Spiritual Life. Note down areas of satisfaction, and of dissatisfaction. Ask yourself how you can increase your wellbeing in each area. Jot down ideas as they come to you and add to these later if necessary.

Exercise 3. The eleventh hour

Have you experienced a solution to a problem that seemed insoluble? In your journal, note down any times when help appeared just as you 'gave up.' Did this come through a shift in perspective within yourself, or through another person?

Exercise 4. Connecting

Look at the collage that you created as an illustration of your life for Chapter 1. You selected the images intuitively, using your 'right brain.' The interpretation was aided by your 'left brain' thought-processes. Note down any changes that have occurred in your life since you created your collage. How do you feel about your life at this moment?

SAM PARNIA

INTRODUCTION TO DR. SAM PARNIA

Doctor Sam Parnia graduated from Guys and St. Thomas' medical schools in London. At the time of this interview, Sam was a Specialist Registrar in Internal and Respiratory Medicine at Southampton General Hospital, and also a British Lung Foundation Clinical Research Fellow working towards a PhD in the molecular biology of asthma. Between 1998 and 1999 he was a member of the Southampton University Trust Hospitals Resuscitation Committee. Sam is now associate professor of Medicine at the NYU Langone Medical Center where he is also director of research into cardiopulmonary resuscitation. In the United Kingdom, he is director of the Human Consciousness Project at the University of Southampton. Sam is the author of *What Happens When We Die: A Ground-breaking Study Into the Nature of Life and Death*, *Erasing Death*, and *The Lazarus Effect*.

While working on the medical and coronary care units of Southampton General Hospitals, he and Dr. Peter Fenwick set up the first scientific study of Near Death Experiences in the UK and also later on set up Horizon Research Foundation. This is a charity aimed at increasing research into understanding the human mind at the end of life, educating the medical profession and the general public as well as providing support for patients who have experienced near death experiences.

You can find more information at the Foundation website www.horizon-research.co.uk.

SAM PARNIA

My interest in near death experiences has gone through different stages. When I was about 15 or 16 years old, someone gave me a copy of Raymond Moody's book *Life After Life*, which I must confess I didn't read from cover to cover, but I read bits of it and found it very interesting because of the similarity of the experiences he had recorded. It stayed in the back of my mind, and there was some publicity around the subject at that time. When I went to university to study medicine, the area that I was particularly interested in (and still am particularly interested in) was trying to find out more about what makes us what we are; why we are the way we are, why we're all individuals with different thought processes and personalities. And I used to think at that time that all the answers lay in the brain. And therefore, when I was at university, particularly during my empirical sciences course, I worked very, very hard because of my enthusiasm for this area. So, I was always interested in mind and brain, how it worked.

I even nearly took a year out just to study neurosciences in more depth. But I realised that it would be a very specific area, and I wanted to study medicine, so I decided against it. Then towards the end of my training in medical school I came across people who were dying, and particular cases of people who had had a cardiac arrest – whose heart had stopped beating and who had stopped breathing. Initially it didn't touch on me so much, but once I became more senior it happened to a few patients who I'd got to know quite well. In particular, there was one chap in New York, where I was working as an elective student, who I came to know very well. I'd been speaking to him one morning for an hour or so about all sorts of things. We went for a coffee break and had a call to go back to the emergency room because somebody (we didn't know who) had had a cardiac arrest. So, we went there, and I realised that it was the man who I'd been speaking to an hour earlier. The whole team were trying to resuscitate him, to bring him back to life, and they tried and tried in vain. And I remember watching this whole process going on, and thinking to myself "What's happened to him? Is anything left of him? Is he completely annihilated? Is he up there, watching us, like the descriptions of people in Moody's book? Is there some element of his consciousness that's still remaining? Is he able to know what's happening here, or is he completely gone?" And it stayed in my mind. After I qualified, I then went back to try and find out some of these answers. And I realised, to my disappointment, that there had been very little scientific research in this area. So, I decided that the best thing to do would be to actually get involved myself, to study it scientifically, both to answer my own questions and also to answer any questions that anybody else had related to this area. So that's really how I got involved with this subject – lots of questions in succession.

The Horizon Research Foundation is a charity that was formed for two reasons. One was that it became evident, from the letters we received from people about their experiences, that people who've had near death experiences found it very difficult to get help. They needed to describe their experiences to someone who may understand what they had experienced. And although the experience itself is usually very pleasant, some people have actually found the knowledge that they were close to dying very difficult to cope with.

So, we realised that there was a need for some sort of help for these people. And unlike any other condition – like asthma, diabetes, epilepsy – that have their own societies where people can go for advice, or get leaflets for information, this didn't exist for near death experiences. So, we decided to set up the charity, the society, for this reason.

The other reason we wanted to do it was that most charities that exist have a dual function. One is to help people who have the problem, or illness, and the second aim is to promote more research into it. So, for example, the National Asthma Campaign provides information leaflets for people with asthma, and also raises money for research into asthma. So we decided to have the same sort of concept, where one arm of the Foundation exists to help people who want to know more about the experiences, where they can join as members for a small amount and get regular information, and the second aspect is to try and raise funds to help further the research into this area.

The main support available is that people can come and talk to us about their experiences. We can talk to them about it, explain it to them, and tailor it to their needs. We're hoping to be able to expand this further, and one of the things we now do is to lecture to General Practitioners around the country, so that if patients approach them, they can refer them to us. So, we're developing those networks as well. But as it stands, we're really the only source of support.

For years there have been hundreds, thousands, of anecdotal cases of people who've had near death experiences. And when they've 'come back' they've reported being much less afraid of death, less materialistic, generally more content and more willing to give of themselves to others. Reports have existed for years, but recently a study confirmed this – an official study that was conducted in Holland over a two-year period. They interviewed 344 people who had had a cardiac arrest and survived, and around 40 of these people had near death experiences. The researchers then followed up the group who'd had near death experiences for eight years afterwards, to see what effect this had on their attitude to life. And they found a similar picture; that for most of these people it had a very positive effect for them, and that they had described the features I just mentioned. So, the evidence definitely suggests that people who have had this experience are often transformed by it and develop a more positive life-attitude.

There are different reactions in the scientific and medical professions, and the general public. It depends who you are talking to about it, and it also depends on how it's presented.

One of the difficulties that we have with near death experiences is that there has been so much sensationalism in the press for the last 20 years or so. People have either consciously or subconsciously formed an opinion without really knowing too much about it. There's been very little research into this area, so there hasn't been the work upon which to base opinions rather than just personal subjective views. So, one of the difficulties that we have is to try and break through these barriers and explain it to people. In terms of the scientific and the medical community, wherever we've presented the work in the actual scientific context, we've found that people have been very amenable to it and interested in it. We tend to get the most interest when we do our seminars. Compared to many other areas, we tend to have more people coming to listen to the talks, who seem to be very interested and who ask a lot of questions.

When you try to explain it to non-medical people it's slightly more difficult, because a lot of the concepts upon which it rests are more evident to medical personnel because they deal with it on a daily basis. So, we have to make it more simple for the public, and explain a lot more to them. But the public have been very interested. Whenever we've been in the newspapers, or on television or radio, we've been inundated with calls, or people contacting us for more information, or telling us about their experiences. To give you an example, we had a report published in Reuters at the end of June 2001. Afterwards, the reporter told me that on the day this report ran, it remained the number 1 article on Yahoo in terms of hits and the number of times it was copied and e-mailed to others. Also, it generated more than 500 posts to the Yahoo web site. So, the interest is certainly there, and we've had so much publicity from all over the world. Even in places we wouldn't have expected, people are contacting us saying that they've read about our work and want to know more about it. So, there seems to be a huge interest in the area.

We know very little about what the nature of the mind is,

so it's difficult to say what the connection is between the mind and the brain. Does mind come from the brain cells, or is there a different process that governs it? I think that from the work we've been doing, and certainly from the groups in Holland that have been working with cardiac arrest patients, there is a lot of evidence building up that suggests that mind may actually be a separate entity to the brain. That it could be a kind of matter, but a very subtle kind of matter that is as yet undiscovered; that isn't necessarily a product of cellular processes, isn't a product of chemicals moving around between cells in the brain. But that nevertheless it obviously interacts very closely with the brain, and that mind and brain have a relationship with each other. So, with the interaction between the body and the brain, we know that the mind influences the immune system, and the body also influences the mind. To give you a very simple example, if I were to pinch you now, or put a pin in your arm, that physical process then translates into an effect on your mind as well – you'll feel uncomfortable or upset. Or when, say, you catch a cold, the release of various chemicals such as cytokines that we deal with also influences the way we feel – horrible and groggy. So, there's no doubt that there is a dual relationship of body interacting with mind, and mind with body.

But more research needs to take place in this area, into whether mind is a separate entity to the brain. Because it has huge implications. As it stands, there is nothing to tell us how, if at all, brain processes produce the mind, but we do have some evidence that suggests that mind can exist at a time when the brain isn't functioning, and when the clinical criteria of death have been met.

The wider implications are huge. It's like many areas in science – when you first make a discovery, when you start moving into it, you can see a certain amount of implications, but you don't know what they will lead into in 20, or 30, or 100 years time. Later on you see more and more repercussions. It has been the same with every discovery. If you look at electromagnetic phenomena, quantum processes and suchlike, when they were first proposed people could predict a limited amount of future benefits that these would bring. And 100 years later we have expanded their use beyond the wildest imagination of the person who discovered them.

But certainly, the implications at this point are both in terms of social benefits and also societal and medical ones. Social because it will alter our attitudes and educate us better about life itself, and death, which is the inevitable step that all of us have to face. It will give more meaning to us in terms of life and will help us to understand more about ethics and morality. So those are the general implications for society.

From a medical point of view, it would help us to deal with people who've had a close encounter with death; to be able to talk to people who've had this experience, to help them cope with it and be more open about it. In terms of the wider scientific benefits, this research has actually come about through scientific advances, and 20 or 30 years ago if you talked about consciousness there would have been very little interest. Science has advanced in that time. We now have the Human Genome Project that's been set out laboriously over the last few years, and potentially we can now manipulate genes – both human and animal – and change them into an organism of a different form. The cloning of Dolly the sheep was just the beginning. This has led to huge ethical dilemmas. Where does the sanctity of human life lie? How far can we manipulate genes without manipulating the person? What *is* it within the organism that makes the individual what they are? What is the mind? What is consciousness? Because, at the end of the day, that's what really matters to us.

To give you an example, there was a report on the BBC about an American neurosurgeon who had performed an operation to transplant a brain from one monkey to another. It was preliminary work and had minor success in that the monkey survived for a few days afterwards. The problem with that is that if this technique then becomes more refined in the future (which I'm sure it will eventually), we'll be left with a huge dilemma. Because on the one hand you could treat disabling brain diseases like strokes, Alzheimers, Parkinsons, Multiple Sclerosis, with a procedure similar to heart or kidney transplant. But you're left with a big ethical dilemma, which is … if my brain was to be put into another person's body, what does that person become? Do I transplant my self with it? Do I take my mind and consciousness with the brain? Or is it possibly separate? So, will that person become me, in effect? And hence, will I become immortal then? Because at every stage I could have my brain transplanted.

Or, if we were to clone 1,000 people, and bring them up in exactly the same environment as part of a scientific study, would they all turn out to be exactly the same people? Or would they turn out to be like identical twins, who look the same, but have completely different personalities?

In science today, cells are being taken from the very early embryonic stages of pigs, which have the potential to become any organ, and these are being transplanted into human brains to grow into brain tissue. And that raises the question of what you will be left with. Have you got 95% man, and 5% pig? And if those cells grow into larger chunks of brain, do you then have 50% man and 50% pig? Where does the human mind, consciousness, soul – whatever you want to call it – lie? Is it from those cells and cell processes, or is there a separate entity? And I think that this is where it becomes significant. The discovery of what this process is that takes place in near death experiences will have implications in these areas.

If you look at near death experiences it's very interesting, because you have a group of people who have effectively been shown to have no brain function, have reached the point of clinical death, but on coming back have maintained all of their memories. So, when, for example, someone says to you "I was at the corner of the room watching everything," their memories were still there. They still remember everything that happened to them in their lives and have had a panoramic memory review of their whole life. So, memory seems to be functioning pretty well, and also they can form new memories at that time, even though the brain isn't working. So, it may be that the brain acts as an intermediary in allowing the memories to be stored, but it isn't actually storing them directly in the cells. In this case, you wouldn't take someone's memories with the brain – you'd just take the organ. You could see it as being like a television set. A two-year-old child may think that the person they see on television is there inside the box, talking to them. If you pull some wires out of the back of the television, you may lose some or all of the picture or sound, so the child may think that if you damage the TV set, you damage the screen and the person on it is gone. Of course, we know that the television set is only an apparatus to take those waves that are in the air and transmit them into sound and image. And it may be that the brain is acting in the same way – taking the mind and transmitting it to us so that we see it as sounds and pictures. And if there is damage to areas of the brain, in the same way as wires are pulled out of the television set, this could damage the reception – people's memories or areas of personality – but it doesn't mean that the mind isn't there anymore.

So, what we're looking at with the research is that if the mind is shown to work independently of the brain, it doesn't mean that it's something almost magical. It's something that exists as matter, but a very subtle kind of matter that we haven't yet understood. You can call it Matter X. When Newton proposed the idea of gravity, he was proposing that there was a matter, a kind of force, that exists and has effects on other things around it. So, if we didn't know about gravity and you were to tell me that the river Thames goes up and down because of the moon, I'd probably laugh at you and say "Look, don't be silly. That's ludicrous." But we know now that it does exist, that gravity is a kind of matter that is very subtle, but measurable. So, it may be that the mind is the same; that we can see it from its effects, and measure it, but it isn't produced from the cells.

With the common features of near death experiences, firstly, we need to appreciate that, contrary to the image you're given when you read some of the press articles, people who have near death experiences don't have to have all of the features. There could be 7 descriptions, or 15. For example, seeing a tunnel, seeing a light, seeing deceased relatives, getting to a point of no return, entering a very nice heavenly type of domain, looking down at themselves, having a life-review. Not everyone experiences all of those. They might have 3, 4 or 6 of these as part of their near death experience. So even within individual societies, they never are exactly the same. But they have very similar common features.

There hasn't been enough work in terms of assessing the experiences of people in different cultures. But what has been shown is that the core features are similar. For example, a Christian in Britain and a Hindu in India may both have a near death experience where they see a tunnel, see a light, look down at themselves from above, have an out of body experience, see a Godlike figure. Now, a Christian person in that case often sees that as Christ, or Mary – something to do with Christianity. A Hindu having this experience would experience it as something specific to Hinduism – one of the Hindu Gods. So those specific details may be different between different cultures, but the overall experience is very similar.

The other thing you have to appreciate is that when people have had, say, an out of body experience when they've been very ill, what you find that is very interesting is that it's the *same* person. They haven't changed. The thought processes, the mind, are still the same. They're thinking to themselves "What am I doing up here? I'm so comfortable, I don't want to go back. Who's going to look after my two-year-old if I don't go back? But I want to go into this light". And people don't suddenly transform into this all-knowing being. They're still the same person. So, whatever their limitations of perception have been in normal life, these still apply. So, if someone, for example, is only familiar with Christianity and believes in Christ, then it's understandable that if they do see a light, and a Godlike figure in that light, they would say "This must be Christ" because that's what they know. And the other person knows that Godlike figure by a different name of, say, Krishna. Therefore they say, "I saw the Lord Krishna". So, I think part of it is to do with what we see and, as in normal life, we interpret it according to our own minds. So, you and I might see the same event, and may interpret it differently, based on our own minds. That's possibly the explanation for the different interpretations.

The Greyson Criteria is used in the diagnosis of near death experiences. It's a 16-point questionnaire that was developed by Bruce Greyson, who's a Professor of Psychiatry in the United States. When he had collected around 75 cases of people who'd reported near death experiences, he developed a cluster of them as common features and weighed them up in terms of how frequently they'd occurred, then took a common of 16 points and developed this questionnaire. So, for example, "Did you see a light?" Each of those 16 points can be scored as 0, 1, or 2. If people haven't had that experience, it's scored as 0. If they had it but it wasn't intense, it scores as 1. And if it was experienced intensely it scores as 2. Therefore, theoretically, people can score up to 32 on that scale. What Greyson has said is that if people score over 7 (which means you have to have at least 4 features), that's taken to be a criteria as to whether someone has had a near death experience. It's really a way of standardising experiences. If you're using it for research, it's very important to have something that you can use as a tool to standardise with rather than relying purely on narrative. There's another one called the Ring Weighted Scale that's slightly different, but the same sort of concept – devised by the Psychologist Ken Ring in the early 1980's, before Greyson.

The main impetus behind my research is wanting to understand more about what happens to us - as I mentioned earlier, it has really been a big question for me, from when I was much younger. Trying to understand what makes us what we are, asking what is consciousness, what is the mind and its connection with the brain. And what happens to us when we die, or after we die? That has been something that I've wanted to answer for many years now. That's really what has driven me – it's really a pursuit of knowledge.

Chapter 6
The Creative Process

Creativity is the ability to tap into and express the impulses of the imagination. Although the degree of that expression varies, we all have access to the imagination, and we all use it constantly. Yet the essence of creativity goes much deeper than this. It embodies the connection with our source, with the hidden luscious spring that bubbles at our core and fuses us with a pure energy that is transpersonal in its nature. When we are intensely involved in the act of creating, whether this is through pursuing an idea, engaging in the arts, or bringing a child into the world we feel a sense of immediacy, of nowness; we sense that we are experiencing an energy that moves *through* us. Creativity is a force; a primal force, just as gravity is.

SELF-EXPRESSION

Creativity *expresses itself* through the body, the senses, the emotions, the mind and the spirit. We are all creative beings. The meals we prepare, the children we raise, the sweaty joy of working in a garden; the home-making, the teaching, the contemplating, the weighing of matters in decision-making are all creative acts. The creative force, like a river, seeks to find channels to flow into in order to express itself through whatever guise we are willing to connect with. It spills out into everything we are and do because it is part of our nature and is intrinsic to life. Suppression of this force manifests as blocks, feelings of stuck-ness, depression, dis-ease. Allowing it full expression loosens us up, enlivens us, expands us, energises us, and enables us to release and dissolve the barriers to knowledge of our true nature. Creativity brings us into union with the vibrant aspects of our inner being and facilitates feelings of joy and wholeness.

We dance to music, and the music also dances *through* us. Its vibration resonates through every cell in our bodies, causing chemical changes that affect our state of wellbeing. We sing a song, and the song sings itself through us. We paint a picture, and the picture paints us, illustrates us as we are in that moment. This connects us to the rich, abundant, joyful soul-life, and the soul whispers to us through the language of creativity.

The creative process facilitates healing at its deepest, most profound level, becomes it springs from within. Allowing the free flow of creativity in any form enables us to open up, to unwind, uncurl, unfurl; to fully experience and express our feelings. This brings growth, self-acceptance, and increased inner harmony.

OPENING TO EXPERIENCE

The *process* of creativity is ultimately more important than the results that can be seen by others, because it is through *experiencing* that we come to know ourselves. Viewing the results of our creativity can help us to recognise what they symbolise to us, and how we can allow inner connections to be formed and healing to take place within the many layers of the self. Creativity is the gateway to the unconscious mind, and is the guide to the mysterious, numinous aspects of ourselves. It helps us to bring these hidden depths into the light of the conscious mind and to forge links with the superconscious, the energy of infinite wisdom and beauty that seems larger than us but which we are a part of. The holoistic nature becomes aware of a broader scheme in life, and more conscious of its part in that scheme.

Creativity also connects us with others at a very personal level, because the fruits of our own creative nature touch the emotions of others, to be interpreted in ways that may not have been foreseen during the creative act.

EXPLORING THE DEPTHS

Creativity needs to be expressed for its own sake. Criticism, whether this is internal or external, squashes it, stultifies it, forces it underground to find other, less helpful forms of expression. We have all experienced moments of excitement as children when we have created something that we are proud of, only to have it negated or belittled by others. This often causes a fear of expressing our creative energy, a fear of opening up, of making our tender selves vulnerable, of not being 'good enough.' It can also be a fear of diving into the well of the deep self. What will you find there? Demons or angels? Darkness or beauty? The answer is both. They are opposite sides of the same coin, and the darkness can lead to beauty if it is harnessed, understood and transmuted. The only way through this barrier is to face it, to allow ourselves a safe space in which we can play, enjoy the process, and learn to accept it once again. The work of Dr. Natalie Rogers has enabled many people to reconnect with their creative source and has brought about healing at a profound level for the people who encounter her work, whether through her workshops, books or DVDs. Natalie has demonstrated that if you paint your fears, your inner demons, or dance them, or sing them, or write them down, they cease to hold power over you, and can be worked with constructively.

Our inner space contains what Jung called 'the Shadow'. This is the aspect of ourselves that rests deep in the unconscious mind and is the receptacle for what we consider to be the negative aspects of ourselves; our demons, the inner view that has been tarnished by the judgements and projections of others. An absence of creative expression seals up and steals away our sense of connection with ourselves and with the life-force. The pent-up energy of creativity foiled of expression gives rise to depression, feelings of loss, of hollowness, and can reflect outwardly as physical or psychological illness. Our anger, fear, lack of self-love are all aspects of the shadow-self. Yet these qualities have the potential to be transformed into powerful forces for change if we allow ourselves to examine them, to look at the roots of where they came from and see how they filter into our daily lives. Anger can be channelled into creative change. Fear can transform into courage. Insecurity and self-doubt can teach us to find true security within ourselves. Learning to love ourselves teaches us acceptance. Our deepest hurts have the most power to be transformed into healing, wisdom and compassion.

DISSOLVING THE BLOCKS

The only way past creative blocks is *through* them; by recognising that they exist, looking at the causes, and working to dissolve the barriers through finding some kind – any kind – of creative expression. Even going for a walk, moving the body, can help to shift the stagnant energy. Dancing, singing, drumming, drawing or painting helps us to learn to play again; to re-play the joyous uninhibited sense of freedom that we felt as children before the ideas of the adults or our peers around us impinged on us. Allowing yourself to feel foolish and realising that it doesn't actually matter, creating safe spaces in which to explore your creativity with others whom you can trust not to judge, can allow the unfolding to take place. This enables you to re-member, to know again, to recognise that the spiral of life that curls up tightly holding our old patterns can be uncoiled like a spring to allow free movement of energy.

A PERMANENT PROCESS

Everything in life is recycled, changes form, re-minds us to re-member, to make whole. The very air that we breathe is the same air that once swept the sands of the Sahara desert, the Steppes of Russia, the rainforests of New Guinea, the snows of Alaska. It filled the lungs of Socrates in Ancient Greece, of Cleopatra, of the Kalahari bushmen, of our great-great grand-parents. Our planet's ability to create and recreate connects us even through the inhalation and exhalation that sustains life. Our creativity is like the air that we breathe. It permeates us, sustains us, and yet it is invisible, and can all too easily be taken for granted.

CLEANING THE WINDOWS

We are our own versions of the shape and form of the universe, the 'one song' expressing itself through us. We are its eyes, ears, senses, body, mind, emotions. Each of us is a window onto a unique world – unique and extraordinary, because we each experience life through our own lens of perception. The creative energy that gives form to the world is provided with a view of the world *as we see it*. If we forget to clean our own windows, to wipe away the accumulated layers of dust, mud and murk that hinder our vision, then we are prevented from perceiving what is really out there! The dirt on our windows, our perception of life, is the negative thought patterns that give us a distorted image. We might find patches that are clearer, and perceive those as moments of great joy, love and belonging, but often we don't realise that the window needs cleaning, and we consider the *reality* to be unpleasant or murky. Our reality is coloured by our perceptions of it, and the true reality is beautiful and perfect if only we can wipe away the grime and see it with uncluttered vision. Accessing our creative energy, tapping into our source, meditating, contemplating, allowing ourselves to experience the blossoming of our inner nature enables us to clean the windows and see that life is more beautiful than we could ever have imagined.

THOUGHT CREATES FORM

We create our lives and our perception of reality through our thoughts. Thought is the energy that precedes and *creates* form. The strength, power and focus of our thoughts all determine what reality manifests in our lives, how it manifests, and how swiftly it comes about. The speed at which our creative energy reveals itself in our lives depends upon the rate of vibration that is created through our thoughts. The more intense the focus, the more the vibrations are accelerated and the faster the outward manifestation. As the thought exists before the form can manifest, its vibratory resonance determines both the character of the manifestation and the speed at which it appears in our lives. Unfocused, uncontrolled, fuzzy thoughts create chaotic form, an appearance of randomness, a sensation that we are subject to the vagaries of life. Focused, directed thought creates clear form, and the act of entering our inner stillness, our creative centre, helps us to foster this. We become less prey to the opinions of others because we learn self-reliance through listening to the inner voice of the self.

CO-CREATING

The thoughts, focus and belief systems of other people also affect us and impinge on us. The collective thoughts of humankind create a consensus of reality that we buy into. It's as if we live within a bubble where there is a common view of what is believed to be possible or impossible. The collective consensus is that we cannot fly or be in more than once place at a time. Yet there are yogis who are able to levitate their bodies and be witnessed in two places simultaneously. How can this happen?

Their thoughts are strong enough, focused enough, to break through the boundaries of the collective bubble; they are no longer limited by the opinions of the collective unconscious. We all have these abilities to break through. If our belief in our ability to create a new paradigm is focused, we can creatively release ourselves from the old, limiting mind-set.

Our thoughts create images that affect our emotions. And it is a combination of thought and feeling that determines our attitudes. The reality that is created in our lives is based on the here and now, on our perception of life in every moment, viewed through the lens, the window, of our own thoughts and feelings.

The mind is the ultimate creative tool. Everything we see around us is the product of Mind. The food we eat, the homes we live in, the clothes we wear, the movies we watch, the attitudes we subscribe to, this book that you are reading – all of these, and all else, are manifestations of Mind. Everything existed first of all as a thought, an idea. Even our bodies are tools for the expression of the countless forms of Mind. When we realise and integrate this, we know that in every moment we have a choice as to how we perceive our reality, how we express it, how we create it, and how we affect the realities of others. We are all interconnected. The fabric of life holds together every strand, and each strand is fundamental to the cloth. Although our perceptions of reality may appear to be diverse, they are all interwoven, and our creative thought processes affect the belief systems of others.

Even our moods affect those around us. If we are happy, this feeling is transferred to each person that we encounter and lightens their day. An unexpected smile from a stranger on the street can change our perception, and this in turn ripples through everyone else we come into contact with. If we are depressed, we lower the energy of those around us by our view of life in that moment. Our thoughts control our moods, and our moods determine our reactions as well as our perceptions.

By giving ourselves permission to acknowledge our feelings and find the root cause of them, we become the co-creators of our lives.

SPACE AND SHAPE

Creativity is the active, 'doing' aspect of the mind. Mind, in the form of consciousness, exists within every cell in our bodies, and our minds are seeds of Mind itself, the creative and connecting force behind all that exists. The brain, rather than being the container for the mind, is the transformer that receives and transmits messages. We think that our bodies are solid, yet in quantum terms they mostly consist of 'empty space.' And it is this 'space' that defines who and what we truly are. When we look at a painting, it is the 'empty' spaces that give definition and structure to the shapes that compose the painting, and which allow us to recognise and make sense of it. In a piece of music, it is the spaces between the notes that allow us to both feel and hear the music. It is the spaces between the words you are now reading that make this book understandable rather than a jumble of symbols.

In cosmological terms, what we perceive of as space, the apparent emptiness between the galaxies, the nebulae, the planetary systems, is not the 'nothingness' that was previously supposed. Scientists such as Paul Davies are coming to the conclusion that space is not empty at all: that the quantum ether is a substance that behaves like a viscous fluid; that it is a medium made of virtual photons and particles - a medium of light that provides the interconnecting fabric both between *and* within the diverse forms of the universe. This indicates that the spaces within us and throughout the cosmos are what *contains* us, rather than what is contained by us. In spiritual terms, this could be described as soul. Soul contains our bodies and the body of the cosmos, whereas it was previously thought that the form contains the soul.

It is when we enter our inner 'space,' when we connect with a sense of stillness and oneness with the cosmos, that creativity can fully emerge and blossom. We are all capable of expressing the most extraordinary creativity, because we are all containers for creative energy. The left and right sides of the brain, each acting as both receiver and transmitter, enable us to understand both logically and intuitively how our thoughts create the shape and pattern of our lives. The association of the right brain with spatial awareness indicates that it acts as the transformer for the emergence of intuitive creativity, and its symbolic interpretation. The left brain association with linear processes aids us in the construction of form. Depending upon how we perceive our lives, each moment is coloured by our attitudes, and creates the energy that we are focusing on.

FINDING THE THREADS

What we focus on becomes *real* to us. We create it in our minds. If we return to the idea in *Chapter 3* of possible futures being represented as balloons on a string, we need to know which string we are tugging on to draw a particular balloon to us. If not, we may tug first on one string, then another, and will be surprised at which one becomes untangled from the rest and manifests as a particular reality. We won't see how we have created that reality. But if we find the string that is attached to the balloon we want to draw in, then we are aware that we already hold that reality in our hands.

In every moment of our lives we are creating, because we are thinking. Each moment shows us the manifestation of our creativity, both through our perceptions, and through the lens of what is occurring in our lives here and now. If we examine our lives and what is contained in them, and then journey deeper into ourselves to explore why this is so, we begin to see past patterns and the results of past focus emerging. We are then empowered to *choose* to embrace changes that we may wish to make, in order to create a reality that is more in harmony with what we are seeking.

WEAVING THE STORY

Think of your life as a picture that you are painting, or a book that you are writing, or a film that you are starring in. What do you want the story to tell you and others? Where would you like the focus to lie? What would you like to weave into its fabric that represents the fullest, most magnificent aspects of yourself? We all hold within us the tremendous creative force of the mind, our most powerful tool. And the greatest gift of our creative nature is that in every moment we have the choice as to how we employ this tool.

Reminder: Your life is an ongoing creative process. You can choose to express this through everything you do.

Question to ponder: How can you connect more with your own creative energy?

EXERCISES

Exercise 1. Wish Box

Buy a plain box from a craft shop and choose decorations and embellishments that appeal to you. You can paint your box, glue on fabric, pictures, shells, stickers, beads. Decorate your box and immerse yourself in the process. Play.

When your box is completed, write a list of all that you wish for. Include emotional, material, and spiritual wishes.

Fold your list and keep it in your wish box. Read it through occasionally.

If your wishes change, make a new list.

Note when any of your wishes come to fruition.

Exercise 2. Window cleaning

In your journal, note down any areas of your life that seem murky. Imagine that these are windows onto a beautiful landscape. How can you clean these windows? What can you do to make these areas more acceptable?
Note: It can help to physically clean a window in your home. This sets up an openness within yourself for an internal 'spring clean.'

Exercise 3. Re-evaluation

Look at your notes on Exercise 5, Chapter 1, **Pinpointing Your Goal**. How do you now feel about the list of what you most wish for? Are there any changes that you wish to make to this? Which items on this list hold the highest emotional charge for you? How can you further focus on these?

Exercise 4. Energy exchange

Make a point of smiling at every person you encounter today. Exchange a few kind words with at least one stranger. Observe your feelings. You may feel shy about this at first, but with practice it becomes natural!

COLIN WILSON

INTRODUCTION TO COLIN WILSON

Colin Wilson (June 26th 1931 to December 5th 2013) was one of the most prolific writers of our time, with over 80 books published, and a quantity of articles too numerous to mention. Colin's first book, *The Outsider*, published when he was 24 years old, brought him immediate acclaim, and marked him out as a proponent of the New Existentialism. His work ranges from books on the occult, criminology, psychology, and biography, and he was regarded as one of the foremost thinkers of our era.

COLIN WILSON

One of my most basic insights arises from that spring morning feeling I've often spoken of, that sense we get on spring mornings (particularly as a child) that the world is infinitely exciting. This is not just a 'feeling' - we can actually *see* this, like looking at a solid object. But it tends to evaporate when we settle down to the grind of what Heidegger calls the triviality of everydayness.

Again, I used to get it when I first learned to ride a bicycle (at the age of 12 or so), and began taking long rides into the Leicestershire countryside - Warwick, Leamington, Matlock - and suddenly experiencing a marvellous sense of freedom, of how big and fascinating the world is. As I cycled along in the morning sunlight, I would be overwhelmed by a feeling of *potentiality*, of all the thousands of places I wanted to see and the thousands of things I wanted to do. This is the essence of poetry - Rupert Brooke speaks of the excitement:

'...that fills
The soul with longing for dim hills
And far horizons...'

Of course, science was my first love - chemistry and astronomy - and these also brought that sense of infinite mystery, and the possibility of endless discovery - at 13, my hero was Einstein, and I hoped to become his successor.

But to return to the basic insight; 99% of human beings are inclined to accept that the wild optimism is an illusion, a bit like falling in love and then discovering that the beloved is, after all, a quite ordinary person. But geniuses can't settle for this. The Shelleys and Keatses and Rupert Brookes' are possessed by a conviction that the spring morning feeling is a glimpse of the truth. Of course, they may also plunge into pessimism, as Shelley did (*this dim, vast vale of tears*), or Shakespeare (*out, brief candle*).

In *The Outsider* I felt strongly that it ought to be possible to maintain the optimism, if it *is* based on reality, not on illusion. So, although I could be counted as an existentialist thinker, I differed quite basically from Heidegger, Sartre and Camus. I did *not* agree with Camus that life is like everlastingly rolling a rock uphill and watching it roll down again, or like Sartre that man is a useless passion. What I came to do was develop a new and optimistic type of existentialism.

The American psychologist Abraham Maslow provided me with an important key with his concept of the Peak Experience, the sudden experience of sudden, overwhelming happiness that comes to all healthy people. The Peak Experience is not a mystical experience; it springs out of *health*, and Maslow discovered that all healthy people have them with a fair degree of frequency. A typical example is his story of the young mother who was eating breakfast with her husband and children when she suddenly thought 'My God, aren't I lucky!', and went into the Peak Experience. Maslow also learned that as his students talked to each other about Peak Experiences, they began having Peak Experiences all the time, as if they had taught their minds how to do it. Briefly, it struck me that happiness, optimism, efficiency, are the natural and normal state of human consciousness, and that gloom and self doubt and pessimism are merely a sign that someone has failed to understand what reality is all about.

One of my fundamental distinctions is between what one might call the bird's eye view and the worm's eye view. Poems like Shelley's *Ode To The West Wind* or *Ode To A Skylark* are obviously written from a bird's eye view, as if the poet's mind is soaring above the world. Sartre and Schopenhauer are grounded, stuck in the worm's eye view. (Beckett is the worst of all). These two views of reality have been battling it out since the late 18th century, as I demonstrated in '*The Outsider.*' The Romantics experienced marvellous, ecstatic states of happiness, in which they felt undefeatable. Yet when they woke up the next morning, it had all evaporated, and they felt that it was simply a pleasant delusion. So many of them died as suicides, or of alcoholism, or TB, or in accidents (like Shelley). This is what Carlyle meant when he spoke of Eternal Yes versus Eternal No.

I suppose I was fortunate in that the problems of my teenage years - a despairing feeling that I was likely to waste my life working in factories, like my father and brother - had toughened me. I have often noted that writers who had a hard struggle - like Dickens, Shaw, Wells - emerged as optimists, while the 'fortunate' middle-class writers, like Proust and Galsworthy and Greene and Waugh (and Beckett) carried a lifelong burden of gloom and self-doubt. This was the true basis of my optimism. I am an optimist by temperament, an enthusiast about ideas, and I often achieve this feeling of a bird's eye view. As a teenager, it came from science as well as poetry and music. When I was 18, the concept of Outsiders came to me as I was reading my favourite writers, and I began slotting the writers - from Keats to Hemingway and Eliot and Dostoevsky - into these categories. That is the way my mind works. But while I was reading the people who went into *The Outsider* I was also absorbed in the mystics, like Meister Eckhart, Suso, St John of the Cross, the Cloud of Unknowing, and Hindu and Buddhist scriptures (the Bhagavad Gita was particularly influential).

The discovery of Toynbee's *Study Of History* suddenly showed me how I could weave these into a sequel to *The Outsider (Religion And The Rebel,* originally to be called simply *The Rebel).*

I should explain that I have a kind of cross-referencing mind. One evening in the autumn of 1954, I was walking along the Embankment with my friend Bill Hopkins and explaining to him what my work-in-progress, the novel *Ritual In The Dark*, was about. I explained that it had 3 central characters, (1) the hero, an intellectual Outsider, who has great control over his intellect, but not of his body or emotions, (2) an emotional Outsider, a painter, who has great control of his emotions, but not of his intellect or body, and (3) a physical Outsider (the murderer) who has control over his body (he is based on the dancer Nijinsky) but not of his emotions or intellect. I mentioned to him that Dostoevsky had adopted a similar scheme in *The Brothers Karamazov* with Ivan, Mitya and Alyosha. You might say that all three, combined together, would make a complete human being.

At that time I was spending my days working in the British Museum Reading Room, writing my first novel *Ritual In The Dark*, and my evenings as a washer-up in a Coffee House in the Haymarket. Throughout the spring and summer of 1954 I slept out on Hampstead Heath in a sleeping bag, to save money, until I was driven indoors by the onset of winter rains.

Not long after that conversation with Bill Hopkins, alone in my room in New Cross over Christmas 1954 (when Joy had gone home for Christmas), I sketched out *The Outsider* in terms of these 3 types of Outsider - intellectual, physical and emotional. Nietzsche and T.E. Lawrence are examples of the first, Van Gogh of the second, Nijinsky of the third. Its central chapter, 'The Attempt To Gain Control', is about Lawrence, Van Gogh and Nijinsky. On New Years Day, when the British Museum reopened, I cycled there (I cycled everywhere in London to save bus fares) and, on the way, recalled a novel I had once read about, in which a man finds a hole in the wall of his hotel room, and spends his days peering through at the people who come and go in the next room. He struck me as the perfect symbol of the Outsider, and as soon as I arrived at the museum I ordered the book (Barbusse's *L'Enfer*), read it through within hours, then copied down a sentence from it: 'In the air, on top of a tram, a girl is sitting…' - the opening of *The Outsider.*

As I wrote it I had an odd sense that it was good, and that, after so many years of struggle, things were changing, and my cross indexing mind made it an easy book to write.

Re. this cross indexing mind: once, when Joy and I were in Hamburg in 1957, a girl we were with left her coat in a night club where we had been the previous evening with her boyfriend, a publisher (who had left town for the weekend). I tried hard to recall the name of the night club, but all that came into my head was Dostoevsky. I began to go through his novels one by one until *The Possessed* seemed to ring a bell. I went through its characters one by one until I came to the name Peter Verkhovensky. Then I recalled that the night club was called Peter something. Still *The Possessed* stuck in my head, and I went through its minor characters until I came to the governor von Lembke. Then I recalled the name of the night club - Peter Lembke, and we merely had to jump in a taxi and say 'Peter Lembke' to the driver.

When I was about 16, I had no doubt I was a genius - i.e. more mentally alive than most people. What I wanted, of course, was to get published, to get my foot on the bottom rung of the ladder of fame. (Although I would have settled for being just moderately known). I got very disappointed as my type-scripts always came back. I had kept a journal since I was 16, often pouring out pages every day - afraid, like Keats, that I might '*cease to be/ Before my pen has reaped my teaming brain*'. The journal taught me to write, to express myself clearly. So when I began *The Outsider* (at 23) I already had style, and plenty to say. Of course, to some extent fame was the spur (as Milton says) - but there was also an urgent need to understand why we are alive and what we are supposed to do now we are here.

I remain fascinated by dozens of questions. For example, at the moment I have returned to a question that has always interested me, the brains of idiot savants, who seem to prove one of my deepest convictions - that we all possess immense depths of untapped genius and greatness. I am always stumbling across writers I haven't read - at present, V.S. Pritchett - and a book called *Frames Of Mind* by Howard Gardner which makes me almost drunk with excitement. In writing this new book, *The Atlantis Blueprint*, I have accumulated dozens of volumes I haven't yet even had time to read.

One more central point. All my work has been dominated by one central insight: that most human beings spend their lives struggling with negative emotion and self-doubt, but that *crisis* immediately has the effect of freeing us from these feelings, as if a bubble has burst. When I was 16, I read *Crime And Punishment*, and, in the Introduction, about how Dostoevsky had stood in front of a firing squad, expecting to die within minutes, then was reprieved at the last moment. And I thought: 'It must have seemed to him in that moment that life was entirely good, and that when he looked back on things that had made him gloomy in the past, he must have felt: But how absurd!' And when I read the story of how Graham Greene had played Russian roulette in a state of teenage depression, and how, when the revolver clicked on an empty chamber, he experienced an overwhelming sense of sheer joy, I again saw that our fundamental problem is that we are oddly *short-sighted.* Worse, we are like blinkered horses, able to see only what lies in front of our eyes. If man is to evolve - and human evolution has been my lifelong preoccupation - he must concentrate on *getting rid of the blinkers*. That has been the basic subject of all my work.

Chapter 7
Inspiration

Our journey has been leading us increasingly deeper into the vision of ourselves as holons, as beings who are inextricably woven into the web of life through our connection with the greater whole, the cosmos. We are discovering that the cosmos signifies more than merely the physical universe. The Ancient Greeks, the Pythagoreans, had a more evocative term for this; they called it the Kosmos. This encompasses and embraces the patterns of the fundamental essence of every domain of life – from physical matter, to the mind, to the purest spiritual energy that is defined in religious terms as the God-force. The Kosmos is the ultimate holon. Kosmic consciousness is the consciousness, the awareness, of the Whole.

THE KOSMIC VIEW

Our creative energy is both fuelled by, and a channel for, Kosmic energy. When we open ourselves to the expression of this pure energy, this essence, we re-connect with our unified nature and to our knowledge of an inner state of wholeness, oneness, indescribable bliss. All that is necessary is the cleaning of our windows of perception so that we can see that this inner space was always there. If we *re*member that it is the space around us and within us that creates our definition of ourselves and the many forms of the Kosmos, we find that our inner space is our connecting force. It is the medium that underlies what we outwardly perceive as separate fragments. Space is the glue that holds all the pieces of the Kosmos in place. It is the commonality, the permeator, the unifying factor; the 'emptiness' that contains the all.

Consciousness can be expanded to include an awareness of dimensions that are greater than the perceptions of our everyday, mundane existence and experience. The deepening of self-awareness, the awareness of the essential nature of the Self, is the experience of remembering, of rediscovering what our inner nature already knows and has always known.

LISTENING TO THE INNER VOICE

Inspiration comes in the guise of inner knowing, the white flash that suddenly illumines our mind, the intuitive insights that reflect our deep self to us in all its radiance. To inspire means to fill with an urge, to breathe in. This occurs when we are open, when we are relaxed, when we 'let go' enough of the everyday hamster-wheel mentality to allow the voice of the deep self to make itself heard. It happens when we turn the dial and adjust the frequency of the receiver aspect of the mind/brain and tune in to a more subtle wavelength. Inspiration strikes like a lightning bolt, and we suddenly *know,* without understanding why or how we know. With this inner knowing that has no logical basis comes a great charge of energy. We feel electrified, intensely alive, fired-up, accelerated, energised, and momentarily *whole* because we connect with the source. We plug ourselves in.

THE SUBTLE IMPRINT

We have all experienced moments of inspiration, and the feelings generated by these are unforgettable. They imprint themselves deep within the fabric of the mind as shining memories that, when returned to and replayed, help us to evoke those sensations; to stay inspired, and to tune into that feeling at will.

We discover keys to accessing that state. Memories are imprinted on the mind in the same manner as we create prints on a piece of cloth. Some marks are deeply impressed; they leave an indelible shape and pattern when the feeling that gives rise to them is potent and significant. Other, lesser, impressions fade into confused or indecipherable marks if the feeling around them is weaker, or if we are not paying attention to them when the imprints are created. Memory is selective and is stirred by associations, and the impressions made by moments of inspiration go deep and rise again to remind us of their presence at the slightest provocation. This is why, when we follow the trails of what inspires us, we manage to become increasingly inspired, and to transfer this energy to all who come into contact with us.

ALLOWING ILLUMINATION

One of the oldest and best-known stories of inspiration is the tale of Archimedes, a great mathematician who was born around 287 BCE in Syracuse. He was on friendly terms with King Hiero, who, desiring a new gold crown, gave a goldsmith an amount of gold for its creation. The craftsman had strict orders that the crown must be the exact weight of the gold, and he carried out Hiero's instructions accordingly. The king, however, became suspicious that silver had been mingled with the gold, and set the problem before Archimedes. Our hero pondered without success and decided to take a relaxing bath. While sitting in the water, he suddenly realised that the amount of water that overflowed from his tub was proportional to the amount of his body that was submerged, and instantly realised the solution to the problem. In a state of great excitement, he leaped out of the bath and ran naked through the streets shouting "Eureka!" ("I've found it!") The fraudulent goldsmith was arrested, and a new concept in mathematics was born.

This story has cheered countless children struggling with

mathematical principles, and also illustrates how, when inspiration strikes, we forget about the collective mind-set, about its rules, regulations and restrictions, and enter fully into the joyous communion with the undeniable inner knowing that *must* be communicated, regardless of convention.

DANCING TO THE INNER TUNE

Inspired people are perceived as being extraordinary because they listen to the inner voice. They dance to a finer, more harmonious, more delightful tune. And their passion, their infectious enthusiasm, tugs others into the dance with them. The energy of inspiration is like a magnet. It attracts, it pushes and pulls irresistibly, it creates new patterns, new paradigms. When we are inspired, we feel the urge to join with others, to connect with them at a fundamental level, to want to understand what makes everyone and everything 'tick' because we feel connected with everything and life is viewed as endlessly fascinating. Inspiration generates the need to share, to give of oneself, to be involved. It leads to wisdom because the inner knowing is able to flow freely through us, and the act of opening to it allows us to accumulate and distribute more of that energy. We *notice* more; our inner as well as physical eye becomes attuned to the subtleties, the nuances, as well as the surface forms. We become more aware of synchronicities and coincidences; the magical moments when the world seems to shift to accommodate us and leaves messages as a reminder that we are going in the right direction. Inspiration makes us aware that every moment is *now*, and that life is a series of 'nows' that can be lived intensely. Our mind opens to the greater Mind. The holon that we are expands to encompass a greater holon. We see how the layers of life are like Russian dolls, nestling within each other.

So how can we open ourselves to inspiration? The first step is to allow ourselves to be open; to be interested in life and all that it holds; to be curious; to notice the moments that sparkle with their own luminosity, and to acknowledge them. What makes you fizz inside and generates a feeling of excitement? What draws you in, makes you want to find out more? What sparks feelings of intense aliveness within you? Where are your thoughts focused?

If we view life negatively there seems little to inspire ourselves with. We all experience 'the pits of despair' at times, when inspiration seems a long way off, but these 'pits' can help to pierce our hearts and open us to new possibilities once we have negotiated our way out of them. If we look at what is good, exciting, happy and positive in our lives, we find that inspiration comes naturally, easily. And when we follow through on those moments, we attune ourselves more to their energy. Which people are shining lights in your life? What books encourage you to think more deeply and give you a good feeling when you read them? Are there places in the countryside or by the ocean where you feel particularly at peace, regenerated and relaxed? In essence, what helps to raise your energy, your vibration?

Feeling uninspired is not a natural state. It is a message to us that our windows of perception need cleaning, that we are bogged down in the illusion of heaviness. It is a call to action, to activate, to create movement out of stagnation. And stagnation is bred of boredom, of forgetting to see the potential in ourselves and in others; of allowing ourselves to be caught in a net that draws too tightly around us to make space for the new to emerge. Release comes in the form of looking inwards and outwards, of being open and accessible to new experience, to different ways of thinking and being. When we feel uninspired, a conversation with a friend, or reading a good book, watching an uplifting film, exploring a new interest, or hearing a story about someone else's achievement that touches a chord in us can help us to get back on track. And once we have cast around and found a trail, we can follow it, nosing out new pathways that branch off from it. Seeking out the threads that lead deeper into whatever generates a sense of excitement in us is what fans our inner flame and helps it to grow.

MOVEMENT AND STILLNESS

In order to release old, stuck energy that forms a barrier to inspiration, we need to create movement within ourselves; to motivate ourselves to become unstuck. But it is also important to balance this with times of stillness, to allow ourselves to find and maintain our centre. Our society is very focused on 'doing,' on keeping busy, yet this can often lead to forgetfulness of our inner nature. In the midst of too much 'doing' we neglect to remember that we are human *'beings,'* expressions of the greater holon that expresses its *being* through us. When we merely *are,* when we are centred in ourselves, and are unself-conscious, in the sense of releasing attachment to the chattering and opinions of the ego, we enter our inner stillness. In these moments, we *are*, and we become aware that all else *is*. Inspiration can then flow freely, because our connection with the source of our being facilitates the recognition that we *are* that source. Inspiration comes through allowing ourselves to be the connection between the Source and the reality that we inhabit at this moment. There is no need to try to be something or someone. Purely in *being* ourselves, we become the channel that the wellspring of life can bubble up through. We become *inspired*, filled, flowing with the in-breath and out-breath of creation.

Inspiration is so potent a force that it cannot be contained. It generates communication – the urge to commune, to *be as one*, with others. And through this, others are also filled with the same urge, the same energy.

COMMUNICATION

We live in an age of communication. Telephones, faxes, the internet, swift and easy global travel all make it possible for us to communicate with far more people than our parents could have imagined coming into contact with. Some of these people we may never meet face to face. Yet relationships are forged, new friends made, new ideas discussed, disseminated, taken up. Yet despite our access to the widespread written and spoken word there are still problems, dysfunctionalities in communication. At a personal level this is illustrated by strife in romantic relationships and within families and friendships. On a large scale this occurs between nations, cross-culturally, in religions and politics. Many people wish to be *heard*, but not to *listen*.

Our era is one of transition. We face the possibility of further breakdowns in communication, or the emergence of a new and profound sense of unity between human beings, regardless of race, religion, gender, colour or political persuasion. We hold the choice in our hands, individually and collectively, as to the direction the evolution of humanity takes. The power of inspiration is such that through listening to the voice of the inner self, we learn to listen more closely to others; to truly hear what they have to say to us. Inspiration enables us to put our tremendous creative energy to good use, to forge links based on our common bonds – our humanity, our stewardship of our planet, our individual responsibility for our own lives and what helps to foster feelings of connectedness and wellbeing.

Inspired *dialogue* creates the space for the new to emerge. It is a creative form of communication that raises the energy of those involved and helps to expand on the insights that are being experienced and shared. The word dialogue comes from the Greek *dia* (through) *logos* (word). *Through the word.* Logos is also a term for all-encompassing spiritual energy, so the implication is that through words, and where the ideas behind the words come from, we can communicate from our source. Words can be easily misconstrued or misinterpreted, but the *feelings* behind the words, the energy that helps to bring them into form, can be understood when those words are spoken in an inspired manner. The word 'communicate' implies a coming together, a sense of belonging, of community. Creative, inspired communication allows the birth and blossoming of new ideas, new insights, new ways of being, thinking and becoming, and this urge forges a stronger sense of connection both within us and between us.

In his book *Wholeness and the Implicate Order*, the late physicist David Bohm, a truly remarkable human being, discusses the ultimate framework of everything as the 'en-folded' (that which holds within) which is 'un-folded' (seen outwardly, made manifest). The Kosmos is the en-folded in the process of un-folding. The innate creative energy of life explodes into the myriad forms through the urge to express itself. And inspiration is the clear channel that runs between, that forms the deep connection between inner and outer, unmanifest and manifest.

ARCHETYPAL RESONANCE

Within us rest many diverse aspects of self-expression. Contained within the collective unconscious are what psychologists call archetypes; elements of ourselves that have been marked out and labelled as Gods and Goddesses by cultures over millennia. These are elements that reside within the deep mind throughout our lives; they inhabit the psyche in varying degrees according to our personalities. They are the named, transpersonal patterns of instinctive behaviours, sources of deep knowledge that take various forms and contain vast reservoirs of emotional power. These emerge through the symbolic imagery of dreams, and we also 'act out' expressions of archetypal energy throughout our lives. We try to be the perfect mother, father, lover, teacher, sage, clown, and so on. And we also act out the shadow aspects that include the victim, the predator, the destroyer. Depending on our stage of life and our focus, we tend to identify ourselves with particular archetypes that we resonate with unconsciously, and too strong an identification can be unhelpful if we allow that energy to rule our lives. But we can also receive inspiration through consciously tuning into, tapping into and expressing the energies of particular archetypes, through choosing which energy we wish to work with.

A study of the myths of different cultures can reveal fascinating insights into the various aspects of our psyche. The energies may have different names according to each culture, but they embody the same principles. We can learn a great deal about ourselves and our reactions and responses. We can choose to explore the Aphrodite archetype when we are engaged in creating art, beauty, relationship or harmony. We can look to the stories of Athene for guidance in independent wisdom; to Chiron for healing; to Kali for the strength to make difficult changes. There are very many archetypes to choose from. Like members of a committee that sit around a decision-making table in our minds, we can choose which ones we wish to speak from or listen to.

Myth permeates our being. It is part of us, and we continually create it through the tableau of our lives and the film of our life that we star in. Our lives can be inspired through the exploration of myth, and we can create our own myths, our own image of our lives as storied. We can look at all of the people in our lives, and see which archetypal energies they represent to us, questioning what this reveals about ourselves, who we attract, and why. We can ask ourselves what stage of the saga we are experiencing, and how we want to story to develop. Mythical and magical tales appeal to us because, deep down, we need to be able to connect with the magic in our lives. Part of us yearns for the romance, the understanding of the battle between good and evil, the victorious homecoming at the end of the long, arduous journey. When we stop believing in fairy stories, something within us starts to wither away because essentially, life is a magical, miraculous process. Our need to recreate that sensation of wonder and possibility, to tap into it, leads us into inner places where our spirit can soar freely and embrace all possibilities.

LIVING THE MYTH

If we are inspired by life, if we are open and enquiring, every moment becomes an adventure. Each person we meet becomes a source of interest, growth and learning through the exchange of energy that takes place between us. We can find that each day begins a journey into fresh insights, and we learn to recognise, interpret, and take heed of the symbolic messages that constantly appear in our lives. Through discovering that we are the containers of all myths, our lives become mythic. We can begin to vision the patterns within patterns, the way the threads of life weave together. We grow to see that our reality is created by our perceptions of each moment, and that every moment contains many, many layers that all interpenetrate. The breath of inspiration moves through us, permeates us, and finds increasingly more channels to flow through as we breathe with it, feel it, and allow ourselves to express it. We begin to resonate with the knowledge that we are more than we assumed ourselves to be. Our sense of purpose becomes clearer as we experience the profundity of our intimate connection with ourselves and with the Kosmos.

Reminder: Inspiration comes through a willingness to listen to your inner voice. By cultivating moments of silence, you create space for new dialogue.

Question to ponder: What mythic life do you now choose to lead?

EXERCISES

Exercise 1. Inspiration

Think back to the moments when you have felt most inspired. What arose through those moments? Which new pathways were opened up? What generates those sensations in you now? How can you access more of these moments? Find something that inspires you in each day and open yourself to increased feelings of wellbeing.

Exercise 2. Your state of play

In your journal, write about how you view yourself.
Which archetypal energy do you express the most in your life?
How much of this is due to other people's expectations of you, and how much is your choice?
What would you wish to define yourself as, and be viewed as by those around you?
Do you feel that your most important needs are being met? If not, how can you create the space for this to occur?

JEAN HOUSTON

INTRODUCTION TO JEAN HOUSTON

Jean Houston is a pioneer researcher in the human potential movement, and has inspired many people through her books, workshops and lecture tours. She is the co-director (with her late husband, Robert Masters) of *The Foundation For Mind Research*, which helps people to explore and realise their potential. Jean is also the founder of *The Mystery School*, an institution dedicated to teaching history, philosophy, psychology, anthropology and myth as part of the many dimensions of human potential.

Jean is also a consultant to the United Nations, UNICEF, and other international agencies. She was a protégé of the late anthropologist Margaret Mead and also worked with the late mythologist Joseph Campbell. Among her many books, her inspiring autobiography, *A Mythic Life*, illustrates how we live our inner stories and make them real.

Jean's work can be further explored at her website www.jeanhouston.org

JEAN HOUSTON

In terms of our human nature, I would say that the most fundamental quality we can tap into is what is called the entelechy - the dynamic purpose that really is the matrix of the forms that our reality can unfold into. The entelechy of an acorn is to be an oak tree. It's the entelechy of the baby to be a grown-up human being. The entelechy of you and I to *be* ... we don't know what, but once one taps into this essential aspect of ourselves, the essence, then there is a maturation. There's an unfolding of levels and layers of existence. As my friend Margaret Mead used to say, we would start to cook on all burners. We would begin to become what we really are.

So, it's as if beneath the surface crust of consciousness, there is this extraordinary persona who assumes all of our buried personas. I often say that if schizophrenia is the disease of the human condition, then polyphrenia, the orchestration of our many selves, is our expanded health. And so, the entelechy is the fundamental quality of our human nature, which is also deeply in association with our divine nature. It is that which gives us the lensing of our divine nature. It's the bridging between our divine nature and our human nature, as I think. It is that which unfolds but which can never be hurt, regardless of how wounded we may be in our lives. That which is ourselves as if we'd had a thousand years in which to do our human homework.

In order to inspire myself in the low moments, of which I've had more than my share, I would have to say there are two things. One, on the existential form, you carry on doing as well as you can, and serving others as well and as beautifully as you can. But the other aspect is that you're prepared for those moments, so that they do not necessarily become a sustained depression but become *ingression*. They are the times in which you go inward, so that you know how to meditate, you know how to access the depths. We all go through the dark night of the soul, in which it seems as if we live in a psychic flatland. But we also trust, as in the mystical experience, during the dark night of the soul. There is deep, rich gestation going on in the fertile depths, so that the richness of one's human divine life is coming into being. And you trust that.

When I speak about one's relationship to archetypal realities, to an extended reality, there are so many different forms - whether it is Christ, or Buddha, or Athena, or, to my Native American friends, White Buffalo Woman. It is that archetype which is not necessarily just a numinous borderline person, but is that particular cultural lens, the cultural focus for sustaining high quality, a high way of being. Relationship to that is often very important. Also, I always talk about creating learning/teaching communities, something I have tried to encourage all over the world. So that in Northern India, when someone is in a bad state, they say to their friends "Will you be God for me for three months?" "Oh, yes indeed, I will be God for you for three months." They have a community that sustains and holds you, and holds your excellence while you're in this period of ingression. Because we all have these cycles, but they don't have to become pathological. Clinical depression is something else altogether, but these times don't have to be pathological. If one has prepared them to be ingression times, where you deal with meditations, with prayers - your deep inner work - you go deeper, rather than just snivelling and whining on the surface.

With this community spirit, others can hold your dream, and they hold your excellence. We have leaky margins, one to another - we are not encapsulated bags of skin dragging around dreary little egos. We are organism environment; we are symbiotic. My psyche shaves into yours, and yours into hers, and hers into the birds. I really believe absolutely that we are a seamless web of kinship in a living world. I'm a dog person, a big-time dog person (*laughs*). I consider myself half dog. So, I find for myself that if I get very low I can look at my dog and his utter simple joy, running through the fields, and I can be that dog, and, in a sense, be healed by my dogginess. But for those who are more abstract-minded, as I and you occasionally are, I can then relate to what we would consider higher principles - the Christic principle, the Buddhic principle, the Ancient Greek, Hellenic principle. I'm a Greek scholar, that part is very important to me.

This relates to my whole sense of the polyphrenia. We have this vast crew, and the ego is only one image among the multiple images of the psyche. And the entelechy itself, especially if one has trained oneself to bridge to it with ease, can then call up another aspect of the self that is not in that disheartening place. So that we don't have to be just picking at our wounds in that same ego-bound place. I think it's important to look at one's shadow and one's suffering; I'm not denying that wounding gives us access to a deeper place, that we could not get to from a so-called healthy point of view. But there's a certain point at which there are no gains to be made, there's no depth to be found. It becomes a kind of rancorous narcissism, a negative narcissism.

We are a tapestry, we are not a single thread. And, of course, Indigenous peoples, maybe not all, but many know this. We've done a lot of work with Indigenous peoples, and we find that the polyphrenic aspect of the self is natural. Sometimes they call it Totem Reality, access to your totem.

I chose this way of living my life. There is a choice. Some people back away from options, opportunities. And for the most part, I would say that I did not. Now that doesn't mean that it doesn't land you in the soup - like being on the front page of every newspaper in the world for something that never happened! (*laughs*).

But I truly believe that this is one of the most interesting, if not the most important time in human history. I often say that other times in history thought that they were 'it', but they were wrong - this is 'it'. For the first time in human history, most of the big problems of the world, ecology etc., are human-designed. And most of the big solutions will have to be from humanity. Einstein said that the consciousness that created the problem cannot be the same consciousness that solves it, and I think that's why I feel driven to do as much work as I can before I die, to help people to find another order of consciousness that can deal with these stupendous problems. Because we could lose ourselves on the earth - though the earth could continue for the next several hundred years very easily at the present continuum.

And what can one person do? Well, there was a study not

long ago that showed that one socially responsible person (teachers, counsellors etc.) affects anywhere between 2 and 6 million people. And then that goes out, and out, and out. It's like the small world hypothesis, there's six degrees of separation, and it's true. I'm meeting people who know me on Glastonbury Tor, and then you begin to see all these different webs that just go on and on - it's not just myself, it's other people around this area of work, too.

I'm ultimately hopeful. One of the reasons that I'm hopeful is because I travel so much, and I do see things that the Press does not report - the Press often goes in for the story that will get the adrenaline rushing and make people buy the paper. But they're not there for the aftermath of the disaster, or the breakdown, or the cholera epidemic where often I have been, in the middle of wars. And you see people getting together and helping each other, the rise of voluntarism, the rise of women to full partnership with men in the whole agenda of human affairs, which is going to change everything. This is probably the biggest and most important change in human history as far as we know it. They don't see the fact that the so-called internet is far more widely disseminated than they would believe - that we are the world of colossal busybodiness. The 20th Century was almost the negative epiphany of all the bad stuff of the previous thousand years, in terms of monolithic leaders, terrible genocides, the trashing of nations by one nation.

Now, with so much information, so much interconnection, I'm not sure that this is possible anymore. In America there's a book about to be published on the Cultural Creatives, by Paul Ray and his wife, Cherie Anderson. I don't know the final title, but its working title is '*The Integral Culture*'. In America there are 50 million of these people who are part of the Green movements, the Ecology movements, the Human Development movements. Now that's 50 million in America alone, and it's also true throughout the world. And luckily, it's laughed at, and that's important. Because as Schaumacher said, if you want to do real work, be beneath the line of contempt. Because if you're beneath the line of contempt, you can get away and do an awful lot of interesting things, you can *do* something. And so, I think that's what has happened. The public media may laugh at all these New Agers, all these Green people - but that means that they're not given the attention that they really merit. And so again, beneath the surface crust of culture, these tremendous movements are going on, which I see *everywhere.* And that's why I'm ultimately hopeful. Because I see another world going on, beneath the one that's reported on. Voluntarism, rise of women, *deep* concern about the earth, and people in small and large ways trying to do something about it. A new physics that gives the symbolic and existential affirmation to mystical creative consciousness. So many things happening that really seem to be the turning of the page of history as we have known it. That's really the subject of my book, *Jump Time,* published by Tarcher.

What inspires me the most? Well, you know I'm never bored. I don't really remember being bored. I find each person that I meet a wellspring, which induces in me wonder and astonishment. I've never met a stupid child - I've met incredibly stupid systems of education, and this, of course, has been a major piece of my life, trying to create an education that really works for every child. But ultimately, I would have to say, what inspires me most is something that has been with me since I was very young, and that is a sense of history, and the importance of this particular moment in history, and the need to make the most of it. And to feel, as Margaret Mead used to say when I asked how she wanted to be remembered "She lived long enough to be of some use." At that time, I was studying the way Margaret's mind worked - it was so interesting. She thought with her whole body, and I write about that in *A Mythic Life.* At a conference here in Bath, I said to her "You have the *most* interesting mind, I'd like to study it", and she said, "People have been interested all my life in what I thought.

You're the first person to be interested in *how* I think." It was about then that I asked her "What do you want?" "She lived long enough to be of some use." And I've taken that pretty much as my motto, too. But it is the sense of history that really drives me - I've always been historically passionate, studying histriography, philosophy of history, patterns of history.

I'm drawn to antiquities. But that was there very early in life. It sparked *The Passion Of Isis And Osiris, The Hero And The Goddess*, my book on the Odyssey. But my father, when I was 3 years old, used to take me into museums and say, "Hot dog, Jeannie, Mummies!" So, when I was 10, I saved all my lunch money for months, and bought Alan Gardners *Hexicon*. The Athena I'm wearing round my neck is 87 BC.

That was something, because we'd just moved from New York to Oregon. So, we moved mummy cases, and big statues, and 30,000 books, a partridge in a pear tree! It took us 3 months to pack, and 2 months to unpack. Peggy, who's been my working partner for almost 15 years, is one of America's greatest classical actresses, and for many years was one of the heads of the Oregon Shakespeare Festival, which is our major repertory theatre. Then she left them to join us. She kept telling us about her town in Oregon, so we started visiting it and I brought my husband there, and we fell in love with it. It's a little Athens - the best theatre, art, music in America - more mind and bodywork per square block than any place in the world. It's like an ancient Aesclepian. So we moved there.

You know, I think that if you begin to read myths, like the work of John Matthews or Joseph Campbell, or even some of my work, *Passion For The Possible, Passion Of Isis And Osiris, The Hero And The Goddess*, the study of the Odyssey, *Godseed*, on Jesus, *The Search For The Beloved* deals with it, too…there are so many books out there. But when you start reading these stories, read them as pathways to your own life. Because every great myth or story has within it the seeds that quicken in you and say "Oh! That's part of my story!" And because the Great Story goes through the leaving of an outmoded situation, getting on the road of adventure in one form or another, meeting tremendous challenges, nearly dying or even dying, getting resurrected, finding those things, those people, those allies that quicken your own purpose and give you the boon - helping you get back out into the world. They give you the whole process of a story of your life that moves, and when you find that the personal particulars of your life can be linked to the personal universals of the Great Life, the mythic life, then something in you really begins to wake up. And so, stories are not to be read just for entertainment. In the ancient times they weren't - they were modes of inspiration, they were modes of activating, letting you get on with it. And you can realise that these stories are great codes that are meant to decode your life and bring it into high relief, so that you can then look back at times that you thought were awful, and you can re-mythologise them in terms of a critical wounding that opened you to friendship, to passion, to getting on with it. And you can then begin to appreciate these funny allies that showed up - the telephone call in the night, the book that opened at the right place, someone that you met. It begins to come together. Your story makes sense. And when it starts to make sense, to have meaning, then you begin to seek for even greater meanings, greater sense. And you become radiant to those around you, because you are storied, and thus you can call forth their story and their deep purpose. And ultimately, I think that being alive in our time is about seeding a larger story, a new story. In some sense, the old maps don't fit the territory. The expected is the unexpected. It's almost as if we are attending a wake for a way of being that has been ours for hundreds, for thousands of years.

And so, the thing about the mythic structures is that they are there, they are trans-historical. There are the variations, of course - it's no longer the lonely teenager, fighting past his toxicities. It's all people together - men and women, children, dogs, people of all races, ages, and points of view, moving together essentially to enter into deep partnership with the earth, that the earth may continue in a healthy manner, and that we may take on these huge tasks that have been thrust upon us.

Now I say 'huge tasks', and that sounds grandiose. But, just as I say that each one of us can affect so many millions of people, it is also true that even doing our simple tasks beautifully and mindfully has an incredible resonance factor - even beyond the obvious and the outward, and the whole subjective reality. I think that a prayer or a creative or a good thought that I have is going into the very river of feeling and emotion and, again, that is affecting many, many people. Just as somebody else's thought in Cambodia is affecting mine. We are supremely and superbly interconnected, and what we do profoundly makes a difference.

But it's nice to have a teaching/learning community that you meet with once every two weeks or so. And you can do maybe physical, mental, psychological, spiritual exercises together. All of my books are essentially written for these kinds of communities. They are not therapeutic communities - a therapeutic community is something else, because otherwise you have to spend all your time listening to one other person's troubles, and that's not what it's about. It's about growth.

I wrote about this. Margaret Mead, on her deathbed, said "Forget what I'm teaching you about Governments and bureaucracy. We're going to survive our time; it's a question of people getting together in communities and really growing together. And then as a result of that growth, being able to go out and do important things for their communities, and families in the world at large". Because they are, as she said, cooking on more burners.

So, I know I have felt myself deeply called from the future, impelled from the past to do these kind of things. But also I know that I hold many people's visions, and people hold my vision. And that's very helpful. So that even if you enter into periods of despondency, you know that somewhere along the line you are being held, and you can pick up your vision again. I think that's very important. It's hard to be lonely (though some people can be) in a world as complex as ours.

Chapter 8
Success

Whereas a sense of purpose gives you a reason for life and the determination to achieve what you want to accomplish, success is the realisation of your aim, intention, or goal. It is the development of yourself as an individual which comes through the process of accomplishing what you set out to do, and this brings an inner sense of fulfilment and increased confidence in your ability to manifest what you wish for and work towards. This feeling enables you to draw more of that energy towards you and often leads to further insights that point out how you can continue to move forward in your life. Success is, in essence, the ability to do what you enjoy, to express in your life that which inspires and motivates you, and which affirms your most positive, empowered, sense of self.

In the eyes of society, success is often viewed as the achievement of fame, wealth, or prestige. These are some of the outer aspects of success yet they are not the most important - unless these are your specific goals. But true success is more than this. The essence of success is the fulfilment of your inner sense of purpose. Money, fame or recognition are hollow if, within yourself, you still are not happy with who and what you are. True success cannot be measured in fiscal terms; there are wealthy and outwardly successful people who are still searching for happiness and fulfilment, and who feel bound and trapped by a feeling that *what they have* is recognised more than *who they are.*

Every action that leads to a sense of accomplishment can

be viewed as a success. Looking back to childhood, the first time you tied your shoelaces without help, the first word you deciphered from a book, the first picture you drew that others could recognise, all led to a feeling of success, of achievement, of greater independence and an increased sensation of well-being.

The meaning of success is individual to you, personally, and your path to it is through looking at what motivates you, what fills you with enthusiasm. But in order to experience success, you need to focus first on what it is that you wish for, and then create a plan of action that enables you to move towards it, step by step. You can view this as a road to be travelled, from the present moment to your intended destination. There are methods that you can employ to make it clearer and easier, and the first of these is to create a powerful feeling of belief in your ability to achieve your aims. If you don't believe that your goal is possible, you will unconsciously create blocks that will hinder you from attaining it.

THE FOCUS ON SUCCESS

The first step towards success is to be very clear about what you want, and to give yourself permission to achieve your goal. This means permission to access all aspects of yourself; to accept yourself as you are, while also embracing the possibility of change. It helps to remind yourself constantly that you are strong, confident, determined, focused, and that you *deserve* to reach your goal. A lot of people are held back by the hidden fear that in some way they are unworthy, that they are not qualified for the success they deserve. If you have any doubts, they need to be dispelled before you can move forward. Remind yourself that it doesn't matter whether other people are brighter, more talented, have less responsibility, or more time or resources than you. Your goal is there ahead, shining brightly, waiting for you to accomplish it. By giving yourself permission to believe in yourself and your abilities and potential, you develop a positive attitude that will enable you to see obstacles in advance, and this will help you to overcome them and move forward. This will also enable you to draw success towards you, because the energy that you exude will surround you with an air of confidence that other people will respond to. If you radiate a feeling of neediness or lack of confidence, this makes people around you feel insecure or low in energy. If you exude a feeling of calm confidence, others feel secure in and energised by your presence, and this means that they are more willing to be helpful or accommodating.

TIMING

The next step is to think in terms of a timeframe that is realistic. If you want to become the director of a large company within a year but have just left college, you are likely to be discouraged if this doesn't come about and this will sap your confidence. However, if you give yourself a more realistic time span in which to achieve this, you are working more within the realms of possibility. It is possible for success to come instantly, but in most cases, it has to be worked towards. If you speak to, or read interviews with, people who apparently experienced 'overnight success,' you will mostly find that they took a long time building up their knowledge and skills before the quantum leap occurred that suddenly catapulted them into the limelight.

Where you are now in your life was determined through actions you took in the past that led you to this point. So, your ideas, attitudes, and actions now will help to determine your future. If you see in your mind's eye a variety of possibilities, and can pinpoint which appeals to you the most, you can choose a direction to work towards, and you can focus on bringing that into existence in your life.

Let me show you an example through the analogy of a tarot

reading. At the moment when you ask your question and lay out the cards, the direction that events are leading into, and the outcome that is shown, will be determined by the energy that you are working with in this moment. So, your reading will show the possible future that is likely to stem from the energy that you are working with now. If that future is not what you want to draw towards you, you have the choice to take a different course of action or create a change of attitude within yourself, which will mean that events will move in a different direction. This is the essence of free will.

Perhaps another easy way to understand this would be to imagine that you are holding a bunch of strings, attached to numerous balloons which are floating up ahead of you. Each of those balloons symbolises a possible future. If you select the balloon which represents the future you desire, and pull the string to bring it closer to you, you will find that it is likely that you will have to concentrate quite hard in order to keep reeling in the right string. It could get tangled up with others, which means that you inadvertently draw the wrong balloon towards you. So, you need to remain focused - and with concentration, and the act of consciously reeling in the balloon of your choice, you will succeed.

The act of manifesting is often seen as you moving towards your goal. Yet, in essence, the goal is already there, and your most effective action is in drawing that goal towards you - like reeling in the string of your chosen balloon.

MAPPING YOUR ROUTE

Once you have decided on your goal and set a reasonable timeframe in which to manifest it into your life, the next step is to create a map to follow, which helps you to work out the most effective way forward. There may be a fast route that involves intense focus, hard work, and no time for anything else until your goal is accomplished. Or you might plan a route that enables you to pause at certain stops along the way, smell the flowers, and evaluate before continuing forward. Only you know what would suit you best. At this stage, it is necessary, along with your forward planning, to pinpoint areas where you could get stuck, or which would be difficult to bypass, and work out strategies for dealing with this in advance. It is also very useful to walk in a mental circle all around your chosen path. This helps you to gain a clearer view of all possibilities within it. You can look for examples in the lives of other people who have followed a similar path, and see what you can learn from them. If you make a mistake, try to learn from it, and keep moving on with a confident attitude. There is a saying that if all your mistakes are new ones, you are learning well!

The biggest obstruction to success is fear - fear of failure, fear of not being good enough, fear of change, and fear of how you will cope with life-changes if you *are* successful. The way through this is to face your fears, see which are real and which are based on past conditioning and are illusory. With fears that are derived from other people telling you that you can't do it, the resolution is to affirm to yourself over and over again "I can do this! I *am* doing this!" Remember that these are their fears and not yours, and simply refuse to be influenced by them. If you have real fears (of risking all that you have in order to take the next step, for example), then work them through. If you are afraid, deep down, of whether you could cope with achieving that goal, then look for another one that is closer to your comfort zone. Plan your next stage so that the risks are minimised as much as possible. Then, if it feels right, gather your courage and move forward.

LISTEN TO YOUR FEELINGS

Courage and intuition are major factors in achieving success. If you dare to take a leap, and your 'gut feelings' are telling you to move forward, then trust in your abilities and forge ahead. If all of your instincts are telling you that something is about to go seriously wrong, and you have ruled out any possibility that it is due to fear of failure, then take heed, and make a fresh plan. A sense of adventure is important, the ability to enjoy what is happening as it occurs. The journey should be as enjoyable as the goal, because you will be learning so much about yourself and your abilities along the way. A willingness to take risks leads to feelings of great exhilaration that spur you on and generate more confidence. This 'charges up' your energy and you radiate that more fully, so that other people sense this and respond to it. Some risks are necessary in order to move forward. Others may not be appropriate, and only you know how far or fast you wish to leap, and whether you can deal with the consequences.

THE EQUATION OF SUCCESS

There is a popular idea that, in order to achieve your goals, you only need motivation and a willingness to believe that it will happen. This can lead to a great deal of disappointment and disillusionment. There are four factors that help you to attain success; two that can be controlled by you, and two others that are more to do with circumstances. This can be visualised as an equation:

(goal + motivation) + (timing + opportunity) = success.

Firstly, you need the goal; something to aim towards. This inspires you to become motivated, to strive to reach that goal. Both of these are controllable by you. You can choose your goal, and having that goal to move towards sparks the energy, the will, the motivation to accomplish what needs to be done in order to attain it.

Timing is important, because the right action taken at the wrong time could prove to be fruitless, whereas if it happens at the right time, events fall into place easily. Taking notice of synchronicities shows you the way forward. If you notice an increase in synchronicities or coincidences, this indicates that more energy is building up which reveals that it is the right time to act. If it feels blocked, or that there is very little energy around you, this is a sign that you need to wait and be patient; it would be more helpful to concentrate on what you can do to shift your energy until the time feels more appropriate to forge ahead.

Opportunity may seem like a random factor, but it is closely linked to timing. When the timing is right it is easier to recognise opportunities that are presented to you. A word within a conversation could spark off a new idea; a person you meet could point the way forward for you, or even offer the opportunity directly. A book you come across, or that literally falls from a shelf in front of you, could provide the answer to a question that has been on your mind. There are endless scenarios in which opportunities are revealed. Cultivating a state of mind in which you are alert yet relaxed makes it more likely that you will recognise opportunities as they come.

These four factors working in harmony generate success, the accomplishment of your goals. The equation is simple, but it works!

MARKING THE PATH

An inner feeling of success in achieving what you set out to do is often followed by outer success that is recognised by others. And the positive feelings that you gain from this, the sense of fulfilment, comes through remaining true to your personal vision of what helps you to realise your potential. Expressing more of your potential and being able to explore more of who and what you truly are is the real nature of success.

Each stage of your journey will be marked by achievements. Note these in your journal and celebrate them, however small they may seem. Remind yourself of what you have accomplished within every stage you pass through. Congratulate yourself and see each phase you complete as a goal in itself that has been reached. See yourself as moving forward. Then, in the moments when you feel 'stuck' you can remember what you have accomplished instead of allowing yourself to sink into negativity that would drain you and discourage you. Your journal will be invaluable, as you can look back through it and remind yourself of what you have achieved so far. Look to other people who inspire you, or whose accomplishments you admire, and see where the qualities which draw you to them are reflected within yourself. We are often attracted to people who mirror aspects of ourselves, or who embody qualities that we want to develop.

In order to become successful, we need to take responsibility for ourselves, for our ability to direct the course of our lives to a certain extent. With success comes increased responsibility towards others as well as to ourselves, because the recognition dawns that while we create our lives from the deeper aspects of ourselves, others are also party to that creative process.

An important perspective on goals and success is that the energy you put into moving forward, into allowing yourself to explore new ideas and insights along the way, is balanced by the ability to accept yourself *as you are*, without judgement, while also embracing the possibility of change. What you learn in your quest to accomplish what you set out to do is just as important, if not more so, than actually realising that goal. The *purpose* of the goal is fundamentally the inner growth that is realised in the journey towards it.

Reminder: Success is primarily a state of mind. If you ***feel*** successful, you attract more of that energy to you.

Question to consider: In what areas of your life do you feel successful, or see the potential for success in the future?

EXERCISES

Exercise 1. Success collage

Look through some magazines and gather together any pictures and words that represent what you wish for in your life. This can encompass all areas of your life: emotional, material and spiritual. Create a collage from these on an A4 piece of card or paper and keep it in a prominent place where you will notice it each day. Each time you focus on your collage, consider what you have achieved so far, and ensure that you are open to discovering each new step towards your goal.

Exercise 2. Mapping your route

Take a large sheet of paper, preferably A3. Start in the centre with your goal, and work outwards, noting in capital letters the things that you want to achieve and how you can accomplish this. Add any ideas that will help you or resources that you can call on, and draw lines that link these ideas. Write in sub-texts beneath the bold lettering. Use felt-tip coloured pens so that the ideas stand out. Allow yourself to branch out as other ideas come to you.

Exercise 3. Learning levity

View life as a game, with no winners or losers. What makes life a fun experience for you? Do you still play? How often do you allow yourself a belly-laugh, or a moment of silliness? When did you last fly a kite, or play a game of chase? Resolve to release fears of looking silly, and do something that gave you pleasure in the past.

NATALIE ROGERS

INTRODUCTION TO NATALIE ROGERS ©

Natalie Rogers, Ph.D., (October 9th 1928 to October 17th 2015) was a pioneer in expressive arts therapy. Natalie was an author, artist, psychotherapist and group facilitator. She founded and was faculty Emeritus of the Person-Centred Expressive Therapy Institute, Cotati, California. Natalie has taken this training to Europe, Russia, Latin America, Japan as well as the United States.

Her first book, *Emerging Woman: A Decade of Midlife Transitions* is a personal/political statement of her life between age 40 and 60. *The Creative Connection: Expressive Arts as Healing* documents her work in person-centred counselling. Natalie was a full professor (adjunct) at the California Institute of Integral Studies, the Institute of Transpersonal Psychology, and Distinguished Consulting Faculty at Saybrook Graduate School. In 1998, Natalie received the first Lifetime Achievement Award from the International Expressive Arts Therapy Association for being 'a pioneer in the field of integrative arts therapy, education and consultation'.

Natalie is the daughter of Carl Rogers, one of the founders of the humanistic psychology movement, and is the executor of his published works. She has produced a CD-ROM titled: *Carl Rogers: A Daughter's Tribute.*

Further information is available on her website: http://www.nrogers.com

NATALIE ROGERS

The arts are a language. A language to connect with our inner self, and a language to express our feelings and thoughts to other people - whether it's our therapist, or a group, or the world. It's what I call 'tapping into the universal unconscious', or the Great Spirit, or the universal spirit, depending on what your belief system is. But we have to find ways for people to tap into their highest or deepest sense of consciousness: their humanity. I have always found that whenever we go into our own deepest self, our own inner essence, we connect to the universal spirit, or to all of humanity.

The creative process itself is healing. In many situations, not just the current world one, I have found that just doing the art – creating a collage, or piece of clay, or a song or movement that expresses this agony, this despair – helps to heal it. But as time goes on (it may take a day, or weeks, or months), you move through the next painting, and the next, and eventually you find a sense of hope, of heart, of caring, of love.

Actually that's one of the things that happened in the art that I just created. I ended up with a big yellow heart with green vines growing through it. I know that through this process I eventually get into my deepest soul sense, which opens my heart and brings forth my desire to heal the planet and myself.

Personal growth and our higher states of consciousness are achieved through self-awareness, self-understanding and insight. These qualities are achieved by delving into the emotions and feelings. Of course, it can be feelings of joy, ecstasy, sensuality, sexuality – all the yummy things (*laughs*). All of those feelings are an energy source that can be channelled into the expressive arts. As you've mentioned, often we don't really understand what our art is about until we put it out there and look at it. I ask people to dance their art, or write about it, or have a dialogue with it. That brings further depth of understanding to the individual. You have the art speak to you. If you have a clay piece, you ask it, "What message do you have for me?" Or if you have a colour or shape, or a figure in your drawing or painting, then you ask, "What do you wish to say to me?" That helps you to gain insight.

I grew up in a very creative, non-judgemental household. As a child I felt very supported in my creativity, particularly by my mother, who was an artist. She created the opportunity for both my brother and me to use art as a way of expressing ourselves. She was trained as a fine artist, so she gave us some instruction, as well.

In my 30's I went to Brandeis University and got my masters degree under the supervision of Abraham Maslow. He was very interested in creativity at that time. He supported me in using expressive art with children.

Also, I was very inspired by Virginia Axline, who at one point was a student of my father's. She was a play therapist, and wrote the books *Play Therapy* and *Dibs* (a case study). I watched her do client-centred play therapy through a one-way mirror when I was a college student, and at home on vacation. I said to myself, "That's what I want to do. I want to become a client-centred play therapist." So my master's thesis was working with children, and helping them use the arts as self-expression, rather than 'teaching' them art. I asked them to work with their dreams and feelings. Abe Maslow was helpful in this project.

Later I began my private practice, and was seeing adults. I wanted to integrate all of the processes that were helpful in my life into my work with clients. That included movement as well as art. This was during the 60's before the term "expressive arts" was being used. At that time there was traditional, analytic art therapy. I didn't know of any humanistic art therapy sources. I really just experimented with using art as a language between my clients and me. It was awkward at first, wondering whether they would be interested in using visual art, like colour, to say what they were feeling. I knew that as long as I followed the client-centred principles, of respecting the individual for his or her own interpretation of their art I would be respecting their ability to understand themselves. (I never interpret people's art and I ask my students to honour that practice.) By following these person-centred principles I knew I wouldn't be doing anybody any harm. And that was very true. I discovered by practice that this was very helpful to clients. There were so many feelings that could not be expressed in words, but were simply expressed through a few lines, or gestures. I could really understand the client at a deeper level by listening to their art, and their movement, and their creative writing. It was my client's positive feedback that kept me learning and trying new ways to encourage their creative expression.

That was the beginning. Then I moved to California and I enrolled in movement training with Anna Halprin and art therapy training with Janie Rhyne. I incorporated what I was learning into my very basic client-centred training that I learned from my father. To me, what is so important is the person-centred philosophy - that each individual has the capacity for self-direction, if given the proper environment. Carl had a deep trust in the human organism as being capable of growing itself if we give it the right environment. I call it *the fertile field theory*. Each person is a seed. If we create the proper soil, fertilise it, water it, and nurture it, that person will grow into his or her own potential - whether it's a redwood tree, a peach tree, a sunflower, or a cactus plant (*laughs*). But each person will truly come into his or her own full bloom. Our role is to create the environment of acceptance, love, permission, and stimulation, to foster creativity. What my Dad didn't do was offer materials and experiences that would allow people to get out of their chairs to engage in something non-verbal. There was no opportunity to actually experience the creative process in those groups or in the client-counsellor relationship. You could talk about wanting to be creative, but there was no opportunity to actually experience the creative process. That's where I feel my work has been an expansion of his work on creativity. For a while I felt I was being a bit rebellious, (*laughs*), to take his work and actually create exercises that would stimulate people to use art and movement, sound and journal writing for their self-exploration. I had worked with my father for many years, and taken classes from him, and knew his philosophy and methods very well. I had incorporated it into my own way of being. So, to do something a little different was a difficult process for me at the beginning. Then I realised I was actually expanding his work into this new realm.

My expressive arts work evolved when I moved from Boston to California and asked my Dad if I could work with him. He was delighted, of course. I quickly designed a ten-day intensive workshop. We asked six to eight other staff, who then co-created what eventually became called "The Person-Centred Approach workshops." Because of Dad's tremendous appeal around the world, it was easy to get a huge crowd for ten days. They were international workshops. These were very experimental times. The staff probably learned as much as, or more than, the participants (*laughs*). Day after day, the large group would sit talking about their lives, telling their personal stories full of emotional content – their tragedies, confusion, fear, and dilemmas. As staff, we were very good at reflecting their feelings and holding the safe space for these very personal stories. We also knew how to facilitate the confrontations people had with each other.

However, because I'm such a kinaesthetic person, I would get very restless, and thought 'How can we *sit* here for three hours in the morning, three hours in the afternoon, and three hours in the evening?' So, I finally said "I have a studio room, with art materials, and anybody who would like to find other ways of delving into these personal issues can come and join me. We'll experiment with non-verbal ways to talk about all the personal stories we are sharing, using movement, art and sound. I had several colleagues who were also interested in exploring this with me. It was a wonderful learning laboratory. We created playtimes that were deeply meaningful to people.

We had very few guidelines. We just kept learning from what we were doing. The way to become a good facilitator is to constantly get evaluations and feedback from participants, and ask "What are we learning? What works and doesn't work?" Carl advocated that kind of feedback as well. We found that this ability to play, to use costumes, drama, and role playing as well as using art materials was very meaningful to people.

Interestingly, neither of my parents were dancers or kinaesthetic. I learn a great deal through 'Authentic Movement' work, or through self-expression through movement. I have felt at times that my physical body actually experiences a lot of the trauma in the world. I take it in through my unconscious and through my pores, so I really need to express it - to stamp, and play the drum, and shout, or move in graceful, sensual ways. Although most people in this culture are shy about self-expression through movement, we have easy games and experiences that help them overcome their inhibitions.

I've just facilitated a very interesting workshop called Earth, Art, and Spirit. In this workshop we were connecting into nature - trees, plants and animals - knowing that we are all One. We are not just connected to human beings. There's a statement by Chief Seattle that I had as a bumper sticker for years which says, "The Earth does not belong to us. We belong to the Earth." That is a beautiful statement. I love it. It is very difficult for those of us who did not grow up with a Native American belief system to actually experience this deep connection with the earth and all creatures. So, the Earth, Art, and Spirit workshop is to help us connect. We go into nature on a mini Vision Quest, communing with a particular tree or plant that we have chosen. Then we come back to the studio to create a piece of art using clay, or colour, or collage. Then we write about our experience. This helps us delve into the deep personal realm, to connect with *all* beings.

Play is very important to me, and again, this was part of bringing all of my life into my workshops. As a young kid I loved to play dress-up with the neighbourhood kids to create imaginary characters. When we started person-centred expressive therapy workshops, I brought dress-up clothes, gorilla masks and witches' hats (*laughs*), military hats, princess gowns and other costumes. This has become a tradition in the institute training program that I founded. It delights me to see our faculty using costumes and role-playing. It gives participants a chance to play with their dark side, their shadow, and with archetypal roles. What we learn from allowing ourselves to try on other characters is tremendous.

As a facilitator there were times when I would gravitate towards the gorilla mask, or the dark shadowy characters. Moving around the room I would confront people with this ugly, dark, aggressive side in a playful way. I found myself wondering, 'What is going on in me? Do I actually feel angry at people in the group?' As I thought about it I realised, 'No, that's not it. I am aware that the participants are being too nice, too sweet, and too kind. Some feelings are happening here that are not being expressed or shared. The anger and aggression is going underground. What I am doing, unconsciously (until now) is to act out, in a playful way, the feelings that have been stuffed.'

As I talked about my process with the participants, it gave them permission to be that other part of themselves, the part they had repressed in the group. It gave people permission to play-act or do expressive arts around their rage, or their fear, or their sadness.

Sometimes we create a 'village'. We say, "This is an imaginary village or a never-never land. You may find a costume to create whatever character you would like to be. There is only gibberish in this village, so you will need to relate to people with gestures and nonsense words." Amazing scenarios happen as people experiment with their adopted role. Afterwards we spend time talking about what happened. Each person has had an entirely different experience of this same village drama. We try to figure out what we have learned about other people and ourselves. Often fabulous insights come from those archetypal roles. We discovered that the blind beggar was not so miserable after all. Everyone paid attention to him and took care of him. One time a very conservative woman tried being the archetype of a harlot. She said, "Wow! This is totally the opposite of who I am! I experienced things about myself that I never knew." That's all play - deep play.

In my book, *The Creative Connection©*, I spend one chapter talking about accepting the shadow, embracing the light. It is an important topic for my graduate students, as well. The shadow is the part we have repressed in our lives. Some people have hidden or denied their ability to love or to allow experiences of light. Most people do have numinous experiences, or transcendent, or spiritual experiences. Yet I find that many people are more willing to talk about the parts of themselves that they don't like - their lack of self-esteem, or their sense of powerlessness. They shy away from sharing their inner beauty, or their capacity to give love or be compassionate. So, I try to create an environment where people can share all aspects of their life experience.

The first step is self-awareness. The next step is usually self-understanding and insight. Then there is the crucial step of self-acceptance - accepting all aspects of oneself. This leads to self-esteem and self-empowerment. Often people say, "This has changed my whole life." It is very transformative work. With a sense of self-esteem and self-empowerment comes new ways to behave in the world. People find themselves changing careers - find themselves doing what they love instead of what they thought they had to do. They take more interest in the world, paying attention to world events and becoming active in various ways, because they realise their connection with the whole world.

There are people who have taken this work to community groups, to drug and alcohol treatment centres, to elders. Others use the expressive arts in environmental work, and with children and, of course, in schools. There are all sorts of ways in which this is being applied. It is a new field. The understanding of its potential is just beginning to be felt.

One of the things that I said in my book is that denial is really our biggest personal and global enemy. Awareness is the opposite of denial. If we're in denial about what we've perpetrated, or what is actually happening in the environment, then we have no way of really changing it. We need to become aware of the global problems, and talk about our fears, our rage at feeling powerless, our grief and suffering over personal and world tragedies. If we deny it we get into states of depression and passivity. Becoming aware leads us into our fiery emotions, and people don't necessarily want to do that - it's Pandora's box. But until we actually open the box, we're going to act out of a lack of consciousness. Opening it in a safe, empathic environment will help us discover self-control and positive ways to be active.

To be in an environment of acceptance, permissiveness and support is very helpful, whether that is a one-on-one relationship, or within a group. That is where the person-centred environment is so necessary. There are guidelines, which are helpful for releasing the inner critic, but basically what is helpful is to be with people where you get support for letting go of these blocks.

I tell people that when you hear your inner critic coming up, just say "Hello. OK, I recognise you. You're sitting on my shoulder again, and I need you at times, because the critic is helpful in my being able to discriminate right from wrong. But I don't need you right now. Go away, come back some other time." Again, awareness is the first step. We all have that critic popping up, telling us we don't know how to do this, or can't do that. Each time it revisits, say "I don't need you now. I want to travel another path right now." (*Laughs*).

The aspect that I feel I'm contributing to the field is really that deep understanding of how one art form actually nurtures and stimulates another art form. Although a lot of people focus on one art form in their practice, such as visual art or movement, they don't necessarily realise that movement actually loosens our mind, stirs our spontaneity for writing and painting. And using colour stimulates our creative writing. Integrating all of the arts, particularly if we use them in sequence, brings about what I call the creative connection. I believe I've added to the field of creative expression by pointing out this connection.

This hypothesis came to me when I was in Anna Halprin's dance training programme. I was keeping an art journal - quick expressive drawings in a small journal. I realised that my art had changed dramatically after the movement that we'd done every day. And it never went back to being the same as it was before. The art expression was much less inhibited, much more from the unconscious. That's where I got this clue of the concept that movement actually changes our visual art. Then when I did the visual art in my journal, sometimes poetry would come forth spontaneously. I looked at this process and said, "That's interesting. The movement and the art and the writing and the sounding all really feed into each other." I have a spiral diagram in my book that explains, visually, how one art form energises another expression. I often dance that diagram when I lecture (*laughs*). It's about how we actually connect to our bodies, to go deeply into our inner truth. When we discover this inner essence it is like an eternal energy fountain and it springs forth like arms opening to the Universal truth. When this happens, it is experienced as connection of the inner world to the outer world, and the Great Spirit. This is where the transpersonal aspect of this work comes in.

These concepts have all come out of my own experience. I didn't start with a concept and then try to prove it. This also follows my father's style of learning - to trust one's experience. What I teach or facilitate for others I have learned from my profound inner work through the arts. It is soul work.

I do keep hope that there is a growing - I would like to say spiritual - consciousness in the world. I am not talking about organised religion or some dogma. There are certainly many individuals and many authors that are talking about a spiritual awakening. There are separate groups, and organisations that are moving toward a consciousness that is respectful of individuals. They advocate really learning to listen to each other and to use methods of conflict resolution that are non-violent. There is the transpersonal movement, and activists for non-violent reform and liberal religious groups that are looking for constructive ways to deal with the issues of the world. I long for and hope for a world (this is so important to me, and it was for my Dad, too) where we are collaborative and co-operative, rather than using our personal power to dominate or have power over other people.

I feel the feminine (Goddess) principle is coming into the world consciousness - very gradually, but it is essential. That doesn't just mean women. I mean the feminine principle of allowing more love and compassion and collaboration, rather than the constant struggle to dominate and control others. Even our language must change from the military metaphors - a 'war' on drugs and a 'war' on crime - it is a 'fight mentality' rather than 'Let's find out why these things are happening and address them' mentality.

We need to change our approach. We have a 'war on terrorism' rather than 'solving the roots of terrorism'. The whole language of our culture is so military and masculine. That is my vision: that we will have a shift in consciousness and empower ourselves to come from the heart. As long as our approach is set at 'we' and 'they'- that we are the good people and they are the bad people - as long as we hold that duality in our minds and hearts, there's not going to be a peaceful world. That is why I was talking about the shadow side. We have to look at what we cause, what we perpetrate, as well as how we have the capacity to heal others and ourselves. The creative process can play a crucial role. Part of the creative process that I believe is so important is to envision a future, to hold up an image of how the world could really work. We seem to be just putting out fires all the time, because there's so little envisioning. We could envision a world where colleagues and nations actually help each other. Having power to share, rather than to dominate and control others. And envisioning a world where people really are equal. So long as our whole world is based on a materialistic economy, where greed for material things seems to be the motivating factor, we are in trouble. We need to visualise a different way - a world where we get gratification and satisfaction out of being loving and caring, and giving to people rather than taking away.

This ties in with all the other things I've been saying, because I feel successful when I'm accepting all aspects of myself - which includes my grief, my anger, the mistakes I make, the pain I have caused and the grief over lost relationships. This acceptance brings me to my ability to love and care. So, in a way, this question about success ties together everything we have been talking about. This includes people's inability to love. I believe that happens because they have not been able to really accept and love themselves first.

So, it has to do with self-esteem and self-acceptance, leading to compassion and love for others. I have self-esteem because I grew up in a family that gave me love and understanding. Of course, sometimes I think I'm pretty foolish or stupid or do dumb things. But I had the basic nurturing that brought about self-esteem. So I am able to take pleasure in my own achievements – which I find a lot of people are not. By that, I don't mean bragging, but really accepting that what I've done is pretty good and has meaning for me and the world. It is okay to like those things that you have achieved that have value for you. Some people who have accomplished great things and have received dozens of awards may have very low self-esteem. They may not be able to say, "Yes, I really value what I did." I believe creating the kind of environment for people where they can value themselves is terribly important.

It is also important to learn from one's mistakes (*laughs*). To be able to say, "I really goofed, I really made a mistake," and to learn from those events.

For me, success is really a way of *being*. I feel successful when I am in balance, and when I feel centred, grounded, compassionate, and really able to deeply understand other people. It's like being intimate on a deep level, whether it's with a friend, or with a client, or with a connection to the world. I feel successful when I am full of light, and when I get this inkling that my spirit is actually felt by other people. It is an inner warm glow. Success to me is about the way I *am* in the world, not about what I have done.

Chapter 9
Creating A New Reality

Before we explore how you can create the life that you dream of, we need to look briefly at one of the deepest, most profound questions that we can ask: What is reality? There are various levels to this. In the context of our journey through the exploration of the self, it is necessary to look at what our reality is at this moment, how we feel about it, whether it is what we would wish it to be. But, in order to do this, we also need to think about the nature of reality at the collective scale, the global scale, and the Kosmic scale.

EXAMINING THE FABRIC

The first step is to look at your life, here and now. What does the fabric of your life consist of? What appear to be the strongest, brightest threads that run through it? How do you *feel* about your life? Is there anything that you would change, given the choice? Who are the people around you? What messages do they have for you? What do they represent to you? What do you feel that you have come here to learn, and do? And are you fulfilling that urge in your life?

Our reality is where our attention rests; it is what we are focusing on. And each of us experiences reality differently, subjectively, relatively, because our perceptions vary. In our comparatively affluent society, a bowl of plain brown rice a day for our main meal would be considered unsatisfactory. Yet to a starving person this would be a feast and would be given thanks for. Our perspective is what makes us happy or sad, despairing or fulfilled, and what creates that perspective is our perception and the emotional reaction that is generated by it. We always have a choice.

We are the sum of our memories, our self-perceptions, our experiences, and how we relate to these. In every moment, we have the ability to create change, through examining our patterns and making a conscious choice about whether we wish to continue these, or to release them, move on, and allow our *en*folded potential to *un*fold.

CHOOSING OUR REALITY

Our senses are our windows onto the world. What we see, perceive, feel, is our reality. Each of us lives within a reality that we create, and through changing our views of it, our perceptions of it, we can change that reality. If our view of the world is negative, we notice negativity all around us; we create what we expect to see. If we view the world as a place of wonder and beauty, we notice and experience wonder and beauty because that is what we expect to see. In every moment we are the creators of our lives, of our reality, through our focus; through where we place our attention, through what we perceive and make ourselves aware of. Our reality is a thoughtform, based on what we expect to see and what we are open to perceiving. This is created through our memories, our attitudes, our programming since birth. We are the collection in motion of our past experiences, thoughts, beliefs. If we change the programming, we change the perception of reality.

The surface mind sifts, dissects, catalogues, creates filing systems in which to keep ideas and knowledge. The deeper Mind expands, encompasses, holds our potential, contains all and allows it to *be*, without judgement or opinions. It simply rests in itself. We can choose what we wish to relate to – the surface mind that chatters away ceaselessly and keeps our attention flitting from one thing to another; or to the Mind, which holds the silence in which everything is contained, that cannot be verbalised, but only *experienced.* This is the *real* you and I, the core of our being. It is our source, which is a state of *beingness*, of absolute love and acceptance. Connecting (reconnecting) with that Source and realising that this is our Self at its most fundamental state, enables us to perceive that this is the reality that underlies and underpins every other reality. In essence, there is no separation.

Yet even with the knowledge that this is our natural state, we still live in the world. We can *be* in the world, yet not *of* it – living our lives in the here and now, while also knowing that there is a larger perspective, that this is only a fraction of our true nature. The Zen koans are designed to help the mind to free itself, to encourage us to enter an inner space where logical thought is not the way to solution, and the illusion is shattered. Knowing takes the place of thinking, this is the ultimate reality.

COLLECTIVE REALITY

We live in a world that is dominated by the collective mind. We subscribe to a certain view of reality because we are told that it is true, that it is real. Our collective reality is like the image of the Venn diagram that we explored in Chapter 1, in which our realities intersect with each other. Yet, even with this state of affairs, each of us has our own unique view that is affected by the views of others but is still our own. The extraordinary and profound *Matrix* films struck a massive chord that resonated like a shock-wave through many, many minds when they first came out, because they ask the question "What is reality?" They helped to shift people's perceptions about whether we are trapped in a dreamworld, with no power over our lives, fodder to the shadow aspects of the psyche; or whether we can wake up, and realise that we are only limited if we allow ourselves to think we are.

MANIFESTATION

So, if we are continually in the process of creating our personal reality, why is it that sometimes what we wish for comes into our lives, and sometimes it doesn't? In every moment an infinite number of possibilities, of realities, are present because we contain them all. Through the medium of the programming we have taken on and are constantly updating, we make selective choices based on what we *believe* is possible or not possible. If we lack belief, then no amount of hoping, visualising or affirming will draw what we aim for into our lives. We have to *know* in every fibre of our being that we can create what we choose to embrace. These many possible realities can be imagined as the child's game of blowing countless soap bubbles into the air, then trying to catch the bubbles. Some of these bubbles float close by each other and others travel a great distance away. It is much easier to access the bubbles that are closest to us, though we can, through purposeful movement, travel across the spaces towards the more distant ones and experience those realities also.

The intensity of our focus creates a situation in which we *collapse* a possible reality into the reality that we are now experiencing. If you watch the soap bubbles floating in the air, you will see that some drift further and further apart, while others gravitate towards each other and sometimes collide. When this happens, there is a moment when the two bubbles join, fuse together while still maintaining their individual shapes, and then they both 'pop.' This is the process that takes place when we step into a new reality, a new way of perceiving the world, gathering to us new experiences that we are now ready to live out. If a possible reality is floating too far away for this to happen, it is necessary to accept, to live out, the other possible realities that are closer. And to keep on blowing more bubbles, creating more possible realities until we are experiencing what we are seeking. Our thoughts and focus are the bubbles. If we don't *believe* that they are strong enough to enter our 'here and now,' they just float away on the breeze, to be replaced by what we are ready to accept.

BELIEVING IN POSSIBILITIES

The creations of Mind are given form within our minds and bring into being a magical dimension in which anything is possible. We are all creators, because we are all aspects of the ultimate creative energy. When we choose not to believe that we create our own reality, we forget this connection with the source of all creativity that flows freely through us. We become infused with others' perceptions of reality instead of our own, and we become homogenised, powerless and unhappy. The purpose of consciousness is to experience itself. Every form that exists is an eye that perceives the Kosmos in its own unique way. Each adds another window, another dimension, another view. We are all born to be different, to express ourselves through our own experiences, while also finding our way back to the source that shows us that, in essence, the Many are also the One. When we return to the core, the essence, we realise this, and see how the game of life plays itself.

The mathematical calculations that Oppenheimer worked out to define the properties of a neutron star led to his conclusion in 1939 that it was possible for a massive enough star to collapse to a point called a *singularity*. Within this singularity, this one point, exists an infinite number of possibilities. We can view consciousness in this way. The potential for the All resides within the One.

REALITY HERE AND NOW

Try an experiment right now. Raise your gaze to look at something that is around you. Now *really* look at whatever it is that your eyes rest on. Know that your mind is creating that image through the physical process of light bouncing off the object and hitting the back of your eye, sending signals to your brain. At the atomic level, your body and everything you see actually consists of 99.9999999% space. Yet in your present reality you can feel the solidity of your body and of the objects around you. You can place your hand against a wall and see it rest there rather than disappear through it, because your mind creates the illusion that it is solid. With this kind of thought-power, imagine what you could create!

At the quantum level, the same component can be perceived as either a wave or a particle, *depending on what the observer expects to see*. Until the moment of observation, all possibilities exist simultaneously. Once observation occurs, a mutual decision ensues between observer and observed, and the form that is then taken on (as a wave or particle) becomes permanently fixed. Our experience of reality is coloured by what we expect to perceive. Whatever we are looking at exists *because* we are looking at it. We create our own reality in our own *inner* space. If the inner space that we access is a place of serenity and security, we can feel at peace in any situation, any circumstances, because our true equilibrium rests within the self; within the spirit, mind and emotions.

EXPERIENCING THE REAL

The external reality that we experience through our senses is not merely a reflection of our internal reality. It simply *is*, it simply exists. Our personal, internal reality shapes how we *see* and *experience* the external reality, because all possible realities exist within us and our state of mind determines what we experience and how we experience it. We cannot manipulate reality, but we can choose how to experience the reality that we find ourselves living in, and our perception and emotional charge determine how *this* reality expands to encompass other realities.

We inhabit a space/time continuum in our everyday reality. Time and space are real in the physical universe. They follow physical laws. Yet every moment that we experience is a *now*. Today is yesterday's tomorrow. The future only exists within our imagination. We can access our memories (which can be distorted by our emotional charges around them), and anticipate or fantasise about the future, but even this is experienced in the *now*. We cannot leap into next week, or next year. And our perception of time changes according to what we are doing and how we are feeling. If we are bored, or are anticipating an event, time appears to pass slowly because we are not focusing on the present moment. If we are enjoying ourselves, or we are concentrating, time seems to pass swiftly. If we are in deep meditation, or under anaesthetic (very different experiences!) time seems to disappear; it ceases to exist. Hours can pass that we have no recollection of. If we are totally absorbed in something, we 'lose track' of time. There can even be experiences of being so focused on accomplishing a task within a certain period of time that time seems to slow down and compress, while we 'speed up,' and a day's work can be accomplished in an hour.

BEYOND AND WITHIN SPACE/TIME

This is because we also dwell within other dimensions of the self that are beyond space and time. These dimensions exist both *within* space/time through the perceptions of the senses, and *beyond* space/time in the realms of the formless. Our essential nature is both beyond space/time *and* encompasses it. Our bodies may seem limited by the space/time continuum, and our senses may tell us that we inhabit this, but the Mind is greater than this narrow region. What we are is formless and unlimited and this is what creates the form that we experience.

Awareness of this can enable us to have more choice in the nature of the reality that manifests in our lives. By focusing *through* the lens of perception that exists *beyond* space and time, in the Eternal Present, we allow more energy to be experienced and released by our thought-forms. Our ideas, our perceptions, have enhanced potency. When we dream of a possible future that we wish to manifest, we need to imagine it as occurring now, in the present moment. We need to fully engage all of our senses; to experience the energy of the goal and our sense of delight as it is experienced. We need to taste it, smell it, feel it, hear it, see it, know it; to involve all of the senses. This creates the bubble containing that reality and brings it into the now. It allows it to be so close that it is part of us. If we are in tune with the deep self, the thought gives rise to, creates, the form. If we are attuned to our higher purpose, this form that we are creating can manifest. If we don't experience that attunement, what we seek to create may or may not come about, because our higher purpose serves our higher good, and delivers what aids our growth process.

The key to manifestation is to create, then release. When we have imagined the bubble containing a particular reality, we need to pop the bubble, to collapse that reality – to set it free rather than try to hold on to it. When we hold on tightly, we deny ourselves the space in which manifestation can occur, and we block it from taking place. So, we release the energy, pop the bubble, and keep our focus on each moment of the reality that we are currently experiencing.

FOLLOWING THE TRACKS

Sometimes, while the process is germinating, we need to remind ourselves to listen to our selves more than to others, to dance to a different tune, to have the courage to dare to be different. If we listen while others express a lack of belief in our abilities, we undermine ourselves and lose the strength of the image of our creative power. Noting the signs along the way, the tracks that the deep Self puts there for us to follow, can help us to keep the focus, hold the vision, embrace the dream. These come in the form of synchronicities and in the guise of confirmatory messages from people who offer assistance, or who may say something that acts as a reminder to focus.

Our experience of life is based on our perceptions in each moment. If we wish to change the experience, we need to change our perceptions. This occurs through understanding what we are creating, and why: what we are learning through this process, and how this can lead us to express more of who and what we truly are. When we understand what our experiences are teaching us, we can choose to create the direction our lives take. We can create the life that we wish for. How we view life creates a constant reflection that we can take as an illustration of where we are 'coming from' within ourselves.

What do you see manifesting in your life? Is it beauty, or strife? How do you view your life? Is it a struggle, or an exciting journey? If we ask ourselves what it is that we truly wish for, how we want our lives to be lived, and how we can shift our perceptions of what we are experiencing here and now, we take a giant leap. We deepen our self-knowledge and realise that we are constantly creating the reality that is there to be learned from, and that this creative process never ends. It is always, always evolving. And that evolution takes us ultimately to the source of inner knowing, where all is as it *is*, and as it should be.

FUNDAMENTAL PURPOSE

Our fundamental purpose is to be who and what we are, in every moment. To allow ourselves to change, grow, develop, evolve. To realise that we are all sparks of the same flame, that we are not alone; that we are all-one. To understand that we are connected at the deepest, most infinite level with our source, which is also the source of life itself. To live fully in every moment and to embrace it, whatever that moment holds.

We are human beings. We are *being* made human; learning what this entails and involves. And, in that process, we are connecting with ourselves on many levels. Evaluating, learning, discovering, *re*membering; exploring all of the parts while we seek to put together the pieces of the puzzle, the whole story. This process enables us to connect with the most creative aspects of ourselves. Through discovering and expressing our deep purpose, we become self-empowered, able to more fully direct the course of our lives.

We stand on the path, here and now. The journey is ours, a trail that leads us deeper into the adventure that is life. It is vibrant, filled with possibilities, it rises up to meet our feet as we travel it. The dance of life beckons. The uni-verse waits for us to add our voices to the song.

Reminder: Reality is the creative imagination made manifest. You are the orchestrator of your reality. Focus and belief in yourself are your tools.

Question to ponder: What is the reality that you now wish to create in your life?

EXERCISES

Exercise 1. Focus assessment

What in your life appears to be most "real", solid, and immutable at this moment? Check the energy around this.
Does it feel positive or negative?
Is this 'reality' what you wish for in your life?
If so, maintain your focus on it, and allow it to solidify further and become rooted within you.

Exercise 2. The bubble game

Buy a child's bubble-blowing kit. Experiment with the bubbles – have fun. See how large you can make them.

- Blow several bubbles in quick succession and see each one as a goal that shines in your life.
- As each one pops, imagine yourself attaining that goal.
- Think of the feeling that this attainment would generate in you and focus on holding that feeling after the bubbles have gone.

JOANNE HARRIS

INTRODUCTION TO JOANNE HARRIS

Joanne Harris is a multi-faceted author whose 24 fiction and non-fiction books are fascinating and enticing. Her first best-seller, *Chocolat*, captured the public imagination and set her among the luminaries of the writing world. *The Lollipop Shoes* and *Peaches for Monsieur Le Curé* continued the story of the central character, Vianne, after *Chocolat*.

Joanne, as her interview reveals, writes books purely for the joy of the creative process. *Chocolat* was translated to the big screen in the film of the same title, and stars Juliette Binoche, whom Joanne had imagined as the central character, Vianne, during the writing of the book. Joanne has also written screenplays for her books *Coastliners* and *Blackberry Wine*.

Here, Joanne describes how the ideas for some of her books came about, talks about success, and effectively sums up the principles described in the chapters of this book in a personal, warm and revealing manner.

JOANNE HARRIS

I write for fun. Publication was never a primary objective – I've always written for my own personal enjoyment. When a book was accepted it was great, but if it hadn't been accepted I would have written another one anyway. After my first two books were published, I didn't try for another publication for quite a long time. I felt that what I really needed was to keep doing what I enjoyed, and I felt that if I really wanted to please these publishers that I had, I would be doing something that actually didn't appeal to me personally – trying to duplicate what I'd already done, making myself into some sort of product, which wasn't my intention at all. So, quite deliberately, I went off and did other things that pleased me. I think that it's the only honest thing that you can do. Because, let's face it, if you are going to write, unless you're extremely fortunate it's unlikely that you will make a vast amount of money, or will be immensely successful. Therefore, the only certainty you have is your own pleasure in the process of writing, whether or not you're satisfied, and whether or not you're improving. That's really what I was interested in working on.

I never really questioned my ability to write. What I did question was my ability (and in fact my desire) to come up with an idea that publishers would find marketable enough to invest money in. My first two books were marketed as horror novels, although I didn't really feel that they fitted into the horror genre. I didn't see the point of genre fiction (I still don't), it just seemed another way of putting labels on writers and reinforcing prejudices; a sort of literary apartheid. However, I didn't see how I could escape categorisation, however little I liked the idea, if I wanted to be in print.

With publishers it's not whether you can write, but whether or not they can sell what you write. This is why there are many people who have a tremendous amount of talent, but just haven't written something that publishers consider particularly marketable, out there with their manuscripts trying to sell them. It doesn't mean that they're no good – or indeed that the authors whose books are out there on the shelves are any better than they are. Some of it is talent, a lot of it is hard work, luck, and appealing to the right person at the right time.

Following the rejection of my third book (on the grounds, yet again, that it was too difficult to categorise), I realised that I didn't want to be a marketable writer if that meant producing books to order. I decided to stop thinking about publication altogether and to derive maximum pleasure from my writing. It worked for me. I found that my energy and confidence were renewed; I was enjoying myself fully again, and no longer felt constrained by anything. The result was *Chocolat*, which I thoroughly enjoyed writing, and in which I gave free rein to my creativity.

Sometimes the idea for a book comes from a specific instance. With *Chocolat* that was the case. I was very much in between ideas, looking for something to do. It was Easter, so I was surrounded by all the symbolism of Easter. Kevin and I were watching a football match together (Kevin's a big fan of football), and he made this throwaway comment that I thought was very funny. I had made a comment about the fact that he was so passionate about football, and that I wanted to write about my passion. And he said "Football is mine, and chocolate is yours. Chocolate is like football for girls." I thought that this was the most idiotic thing, and also very funny, and I thought: what if I was to construct a plot entirely centred around chocolate? The stimulus, the metaphor, the motivation. And I came up with this rather ridiculous story really, which is like a kind of spaghetti western. By half-time I had plotted out the story and knew exactly where it was going to go. This is very rare for me – often the story is kicking around for quite a long time, I'm thinking about it on and off, and I don't really know where it came from. Or something will spark it off.

With *Blackberry Wine* I knew the story was going to be about my English grandfather. He was an ex-miner, a gardener, a dreamer. When he died I had to go and clear out his house. When I went down into his pantry I found all these bottles of wine that he'd made, with labels like Elderflower 1973. It struck me that these bottles were what was left of him, and if I were to open them, these years that I could remember from my childhood would come out. And this is really where the story of *Blackberry Wine* came from. I wrote *Blackberry Wine* as a follow-up to *Chocolat* – partly because I wanted to balance *Chocolat* with something completely different, and also because I had liked the village that had figured so prominently in

Chocolat and wanted to go back there. It was a bit like wanting to extend a holiday for a little bit longer.

I tend not to stay in the same area for long, in writing terms. With *Five Quarters of The Orange*, I started it quite a long time before *Blackberry Wine*. With *Five Quarters* I wanted to write something darker and more challenging. I set it in France during the war, and this automatically set me thinking about my French grandfather, who was a war hero. He was a schoolmaster, and he and his family lived in the school. My grandmother worked in the Post Office, in communications. My grandfather had been in the army and was involved in combat. When he returned to his village, he found it occupied. The Germans had commandeered the school and the barracks. The school was still running, there was a kind of boarding school element to it, but it was divided into two, and it was part of his job to make sure that the children were taught but were kept away from the Germans. He had three very young daughters – my mother, the eldest, was only about seven years old – and his secondary responsibility was to ensure that his own kids didn't get into trouble with the Germans. He had a third, secret, responsibility. He was also working for counter-espionage, working alongside the Resistance and passing on messages via my grandmother's job – all of this was happening under the noses of the Germans. I used to hear an awful lot of stories about what it was like.

One of the things that struck me most was how very different the war was for the children. My mother's stories were so different to my grandfather's. She had a wonderful time – the Germans all thought that this little girl running around was hilarious, and gave her presents. She would go to their cafeteria and eat their food. Even when, later on, they were renounced to the Gestapo and had to go on the run otherwise they would have been shot, she thought it was exciting because they went to stay with a cousin who had a farm. There were all these animals, they didn't have to go to school, and it was great fun. My grandparents were hiding in the basement in fear of their lives, and the children were having a whale of a time. So, I thought I'd write a war story from the perspective of the children not understanding what was actually going on in the world around them and in the wider world of Europe politically during the war. And not understanding the problems of the adults around them, and what they were having to live through. I used a lot of the little anecdotes that my grandfather told me, which is where much of the circumstantial stuff comes from.

Coastliners was set in an imaginary place that was very much like the island where my grandfather had a house. There was a beach that I used to go to quite frequently, but after my grandfather died and we lost the house, there wasn't much reason to go back for a long time. A few years ago I took Anouchka there because I wanted to show her around the place. When we went to the beach, we found that it was gone. There was no sand there at all – just stones and rubble, and these beach huts on immensely long legs, towering over the rocks. You could tell from that exactly how much sand had gone. I investigated why this had happened, and it was very clear that there was a factor to do with construction on the other side of the island. I thought: how fascinating – these people on the other side of the island have actually stolen the beach, and made the sand come to their side of it. It was a great story.

Holy Fools was a story that had been rattling around for a very long time. I had a working draft of it before I even began *Chocolat*, and worked on it on and off, as a fallback novel. When other things weren't going too well, or when I was getting bored or a bit depressed with things that were too bleak and challenging, I would go to *Holy Fools* for fun. I started thinking about the plot for this when I was at university.

At Cambridge, part of the second year was on the theatre of the 17th century, which is interesting because that is where all the great playwrights began to emerge. This was a period of tremendous social and political upheaval, and a time when all kinds of things became accessible. The church was in flux, the king had just been assassinated, which meant that all the political parties and religious parties that had been affiliated to the king now gravitated to his wife, the regent, because his son, who would be Louis XIII, was then only nine years old and too young to take the throne. The queen, Marie de Medici, had powerful catholic affiliations (all the Medici's did), and so there was tremendous turmoil in court, and in the arts and sciences. The king had been a patron of the arts, and the re-emergence of the church, which saw its time coming again, of course tried to (rather unsuccessfully) squash the newly developing artists and writers. It was a fabulous moment in history to write about, because it was immensely dramatic.

Now, what happened when the king was assassinated was that all of the king's favourites started to leave the court, because they could see that the queen's favourites were going to be in conflict with them. And you had the church taking over at a time when it had played a relatively less important role. The thing to do at that time if you wanted to get favour was to place one of your sons or daughters, with a substantial amount of money, in a high position within the church. That way you would get kudos from the court, the establishment, and you would have somebody in a high position in the church to grant you whatever favours they could, if you needed them.

When I was studying this, doing some historical background, I read of a wonderful case in an abbey in Paris at that time, where the mother superior was replaced, for political reasons, by the eleven-year-old high-born younger daughter of a very wealthy family. The mother superior left, and the entire abbey was taken over by this pre-adolescent girl who, having been thoroughly indoctrinated by her mentors, decided that she was going to instigate a reform. And she created her own order which endured for a couple of hundred years and became well-known for stringency. It struck me that this was an absolutely wonderful human drama. In modern terms, it's actually the drama of a new boss arriving at the office, and everyone first of all sussing them out, then going into camps. There will always be people who resent the appointment of a new boss, particularly if that is a much younger person. There will be people who instantly suck up to them to curry favour, people who will be confrontational and fall into disfavour, and so on. It's a small community, and I've always written about those. But in this case, in a cloister, there's a particularly interesting fetid atmosphere because it's the smallest community you can think of, and it's closed to the outside world.

So, this story followed me around for a long, long time, and I thought about writing a story where this could happen. *Holy Fools* was effectively a relocated version of this, with some elements of my own that are completely fictional, against this fairly authentic historical background. I'd always wanted to write a historical novel, but not a dry one with real individuals, because although there are very good, very effective ones published, so much research and proof is needed that you become tremendously constrained and your fiction isn't pure fiction any more. I wanted to write a kind of burlesque, very much in the nature of the plays at that time – the comic melodramas, which is exactly what Holy Fools is, and what it was always intended to be. I had a great time writing it, and one of the reasons that I didn't finish it for such a long time was that I was having so much fun with it, and finishing it would have meant that I didn't have it to fall back on.

I didn't imagine that my work would become so successful. It didn't really cross my mind. I don't tend to be very ambitious. I don't look very far ahead. I was never very concerned about making money or earning praise (although those things are very nice; don't let anyone ever tell you otherwise). What I really wanted was to be better than I was. I learned not to take rejection personally. I had so many rejection letters, and little brochures on punctuation, that I used them to make a papier mache sculpture (a phoenix), and every time I added a piece I simply told myself that I would have to work harder next time. I thought it was quite funny. It was jolly good training, because that doesn't stop when you are published – it just becomes the critic's job rather than the publisher's. There's always somebody who's going to tell you that you're rubbish, and that you shouldn't be where you are, and you might as well pack it in and go home. You do have the right not to listen to these people though, and I think it's something that everybody starting off writing should bear in mind. You're going to get a lot of criticism, but that doesn't necessarily make it all true. And I'm still here. *(Laughs)*. I could make a whole fleet of papier mache phoenixes out of what the critics have said, but I'm still here! *(Laughs)*

I think everybody fantasises about various things, but that's what you expect about somebody who writes books - they invent things, don't they? I was very surprised at the success of *Chocolat*, partly because I had been told in no uncertain terms that it had no chance of success. And also because I'd already published books and thought I knew the way it worked – you write a book, send it off, eighteen months later it comes out in paperback, sells 2,000 copies, and sinks without a trace. I'd learned that already, and thought I was satisfied with that. Just to be in print was fine.

I got a kick out of being in print, and still do. The rest of it didn't seem to be quite 'me.' I love the fact that people argue about my books though, that people have these widely differing opinions on what a book is like, whether it's wonderful, or trash, or ask 'does she stay or does she go?' I think it's great that they have stimulated this huge amount of debate. *Five Quarters of The Orange* is the one that stimulated the most, in the sense that everybody I have met has been divided on this one. They either think it's the best book I have written, or that it's a rather embarrassing blip in a series of rather good books, and they just can't think why I wrote something so nasty and dark. I love the fact that when you have written a book, it is no longer explicitly yours. It belongs to anybody who's willing to go out and buy it, and after that, it's theirs and they can draw from it whatever they want to.

The great joke, of course, is that most of them are drawing something from within themselves. So, I have a good laugh about anybody who says of one book "It was dull and meaningless," because for every person who says that, there's another who says "It's so exciting and multi-layered." People draw their own conclusions, really.

With success, I think a lot of it is luck. I've met a lot of depressed, frustrated authors who are still lugging their manuscripts round and round publishing houses. And I have to say that a certain amount of it is talent, much, much more of it is hard work, and there's a luck factor as well. This is why it's important for people to remain positive, because it's much too easy to be depressed and put off by somebody saying, "This is unsaleable" or "We don't think you have what it takes." We don't understand exactly what it takes. And even something that seemed an obvious idea, like *Chocolat*, went through an awful lot of to-ing and fro-ing and being rejected before people said, "Actually we do think this is a good story, and we are going to publish it." It takes the publishing world a long, long time to come to any decisions.

People's attitudes do change when you become successful. Sometimes your friends just drop you, because they have tremendous expectations of how you're going to change. Sometimes the shifts in the dynamics of people around you can be quite startling. It can be quite traumatic for some people. I think it was Gore Vidal who said that, basically, the worst, most depressing thing is the success of a friend. I'm paraphrasing of course, but you do get people who are jealous, and they feel bad about feeling jealous, so they don't want to have much to do with you because it makes them feel bad about feeling bad.

There are people who suddenly start feeling terribly inadequate, and assume that you will now be swanking around with your fancy new author friends, and won't want to know them anymore. Sometimes you can get these people back on your side just by proving that it ain't so. And what does happen that I find quite depressing is that an awful lot of people come out of the woodwork claiming to be friends, who never were before. They really want to be groupies, and that's kind of sad.

Fortunately, the friends that I have are real friends who have been there pretty much from the start; nothing much was going to change. It's something that you have to get used to, and struggle with it a bit. A friend of mine compared it with getting a terminal disease. Some people will drop you if you get cancer or AIDS or something, because they have this blockage on how to talk to you. It's not because they don't like you anymore. They just don't want to mention the dreaded whatever-it-is that you've got. Whereas other people will actually rally round and be supportive.

My family, of course, have never noticed. It's really funny. My mother occasionally makes forlorn little sounds about how bad it is that I gave up teaching, and now I don't have a proper job. *(Laughs)*. That's about it, really!

What keeps me grounded is my family, my friends, and my cynicism. I went to the Whittaker Book Awards a few years ago, when *Chocolat* sold its first half-million. It's sold a lot more since then, but this was my first award. Whittaker do golden records, and now they've started doing golden books as well.

So, I got my little award, and I came back home clutching it, and went in search of Anouchka, who was colouring. And I said "Look, Anouchka, I've got this gold award". And she kind of opened one eye over her colouring book and said "Yes, but J.K. Rowling got three platinum ones, didn't she?" *(Laughs)*. And I thought: yes, if I ever start floating off the ground, this is going to hold me down. You have to understand that a lot of it is actually crap. It's nice, but you don't have to believe all the things that are said about you – bad or good. Because it's important to retain self-knowledge, and you have to understand that you're still exactly the same person that you were before. Just because a few people have been complimentary about you in print doesn't necessarily make you a better person.

Mind And Motivation Exercises

The exercises at the end of each chapter in this book are designed to enable you to find a sense of purpose in all areas of your life, through understanding yourself more profoundly. On completion of the book you can go back to these at any time and choose to repeat any exercise that has resonance for you with a specific purpose in mind. Have fun!

CHAPTER 1

Exercise 1. Feeling good

In your journal, write a list of anything that makes you feel good. You can score the items on your list between 1 (for nice) and 5 (for wonderful). At the end of each day when you write in your journal, see how many feel-good points you have scored.

Exercise 2. Collage

You will need: Some magazines, scissors, glue, an A4 piece of card or paper, (optional) decorative glitter, ribbon

- Ensure that you will not be disturbed.
- Leaf through the magazines and cut out any pictures or words that have significance for you.
- Without using the glue, arrange your chosen images and words on the A4 paper. Shuffle them around until they feel 'right.'

- Glue them down and add decorations or embellishments if you wish.
- Once you have finished, sit back and look at your collage. Observe whether there are spaces that look 'full' or have gaps. What do you feel about the images you have chosen?

Exercise 3. Interpreting your collage

- Divide your collage into halves.
- The upper half shows what you are conscious of, and your hopes and plans for the future.
- The central line reveals where your focus lies at this moment.
- The lower half reveals messages from your subconscious mind. This can provide clues to inner, hidden motivations, and can also reveal influences from the past that you may not have considered.

Exercise 4. Coincidences and synchronicities

Note down any coincidences or synchronicities in your journal. How did you feel when these occurred? What was happening at the time when you noticed the synchronicities? What did these lead into?

Exercise 5. Pinpointing your goal

In your journal, write down what you most wish for in your life. Then list any gifts or skills that you can use or develop. Do you view your goal as accessible?

CHAPTER 2

Exercise 1. Evaluation

Spend some time thinking about the answers to these questions, as they may not come immediately. Then write them down in your journal.

- What is your immediate goal?
- What would you like to achieve in a year, and five years?
- What gifts and skills can you use towards the attainment of this goal?
- What assets can you call on? These could be emotional, material, logical, or cooperative.
- How can you further develop these? What steps can you take now to realise your goal?

Exercise 2. Increasing self-esteem

When someone pays you a compliment, accept it with a smile and make no comment, justification or excuses. Make a note of any praise or compliments in your journal and tell yourself that you are worthy of them. Allow yourself to acknowledge your positive qualities. Focus on these.

CHAPTER 3

Exercise 1. Winning through

Look back over your life at times in which you have faced a major challenge. List these in your journal. Then answer these questions for each situation.
What was it?
How did you feel when you encountered it?

What course of action did you take?
What did this lead to?
How did you feel afterwards?
What did this teach you about yourself?

Exercise 2. Facing Fears

In your journal, write down your fears. These could be general or specific. Focus initially on the fears that are directly related to a situation that you are currently dealing with. Now take a close look at these fears and write down what you feel has created them.
Have you encountered these fears before?
Are they part of a reactive pattern?
How have you dealt with them in the past?
What is the worst-case scenario that could have resulted?
Did this scenario actually come about?
Often, our fears are illusory. Confronting them lessens their power over us.

Exercise 3. Unexpected outcomes

In your journal, note any situations in which you focused on a specific outcome that turned out differently to your hopes at the time.
What happened?
What was the eventual outcome?
What did this lead into?
Looking back at that time, can you see that outcome as positive, even though it was not what you had anticipated?

Exercise 4. Acknowledging strengths

In your journal, list all of your strong points. Add to these, as you may find that when you are low in confidence, you focus

on weaknesses rather than strengths.
When have you called these strong aspects of yourself into play?
What resulted from this?
How did you feel afterwards?
Did anyone else recognise this in you, and comment on it?
Remind yourself of your strengths frequently, especially in moments when you feel disempowered.

Exercise 5. Sleep-solving

If the solution to a problem seems elusive, write it down on a piece of paper before you go to sleep. Place this under your pillow. Then relax and release any worries. Often the answer comes over the next two or three days.

This is where the term 'sleep on it' comes from. There is no magic involved – you are allowing your subconscious mind to find the answer and bring it to the attention of the conscious mind.

CHAPTER 4

Exercise 1. Music and emotion

Think of a particular song that affects you deeply.
How do you feel when you hear it?
Does it send a shiver up your spine, or elevate your mood, or provide the energy for you to accomplish a task?
Pay close attention to what it is in that song that resonates with you. Music sets up a set of vibrations that attunes you to your emotional self.

Exercise 2. Special quality

In your journal, write down one quality within yourself that shines out beyond all others. What is your special quality? Is it love, compassion, intelligence, perception, inquisitiveness, nurturing, strength, resilience, or something else? Imagine that part of your purpose is to develop and embody that quality. How can you work with this? What results are possible through this?

Exercise 3. Opening to insights

Set aside a few minutes regularly, perhaps once a week, when you allow yourself to relax and drift off. In your journal, note down any ideas and insights that result from this. See where these threads lead to.

Exercise 4. Relaxed awareness

Practice being awake and alert. During a conversation, mentally note everything about the people around you – hair and eye colouring, body language, tone of voice, clothes. Try this exercise at work, or at a party. Afterwards, see how many details you can remember. You can learn a great deal about other people through observation.
NOTE: The trick is to be relaxed, while paying attention. Very little effort is required. After a while, you will find that this occurs automatically.

Exercise 5. Random joy

Each time you experience that "spring morning feeling", the sheer joy of being alive, fully immerse yourself in it. Note down in your journal the time and circumstances in which it arose. Was this precipitated by anything? Can you repeat that feeling consciously?

CHAPTER 5

Exercise 1. Perception and feeling

Pay attention to your changes of mood and note in your journal how your perception shifts depending upon how you are feeling. When do you experience a sense of connection, however fleeting?

Take a daily routine such as preparing a meal. Notice your attitude and feelings during this.

If you are in a hurry, or distracted, does this become a chore?

If you are relaxed, can you absorb yourself in the process of self-nourishment?

Observing how your perceptions are governed by your mood helps you to be more in control of your life.

Exercise 2. Evaluation

As a child, you questioned everything. Have you maintained that intense curiosity? In your journal, divide a page into 4 sections, headed Emotional Life, Work Life, Play, Spiritual Life. Note down areas of satisfaction, and of dissatisfaction. Ask yourself how you can increase your wellbeing in each area. Jot down ideas as they come to you and add to these later if necessary.

Exercise 3. The eleventh hour

Have you experienced a solution to a problem that seemed insoluble? In your journal, note down any times when help appeared just as you 'gave up.' Did this come through a shift in perspective within yourself, or through another person?

Exercise 4. Connecting

Look at the collage that you created as an illustration of your life for Chapter 1. You selected the images intuitively, using your 'right brain.' The interpretation was aided by your 'left brain' thought-processes. Note down any changes that have occurred in your life since you created your collage. How do you feel about your life at this moment?

CHAPTER 6

Exercise 1. Wish Box

Buy a plain box from a craft shop and choose decorations and embellishments that appeal to you. You can paint your box, glue on fabric, pictures, shells, stickers, beads. Decorate your box and immerse yourself in the process. Play.

When your box is completed, write a list of all that you wish for. Include emotional, material, and spiritual wishes.

Fold your list and keep it in your wish box. Read it through occasionally.

If your wishes change, make a new list.

Note when any of your wishes come to fruition.

Exercise 2. Window cleaning

In your journal, note down any areas of your life that seem murky. Imagine that these are windows onto a beautiful landscape. How can you clean these windows? What can you do to make these areas more acceptable?

Note: It can help to physically clean a window in your home. This sets up an openness within yourself for an internal "spring clean".

Exercise 3. Re-evaluation

Look at your notes on Exercise 5, Chapter 1, Pinpointing Your Goal. How do you now feel about the list of what you most wish for? Are there any changes that you wish to make to this? Which items on this list hold the highest emotional charge for you? How can you further focus on these?

Exercise 4. Energy exchange

Make a point of smiling at every person you encounter today. Exchange a few words with at least one stranger. Observe your feelings. You may feel shy about this at first, but with practice it becomes natural!

CHAPTER 7

Exercise 1. Inspiration

Think back to the moments when you have felt most inspired. What arose through those moments? Which new pathways were opened up? What generates those sensations in you now? How can you access more of these moments? Find something that inspires you in each day and open yourself to increased feelings of wellbeing.

Exercise 2. Your state of play

In your journal, write about how you view yourself.
Which archetypal energy do you express the most in your life?
How much of this is due to other people's expectations of you, and how much is your choice?
What would you wish to define yourself as, and be viewed as by those around you?
Do you feel that your most important needs are being met? If

not, how can you create the space for this to occur?

CHAPTER 8

Exercise 1. Success collage

Look through some magazines and gather together any pictures and words that represent what you wish for in your life. This can encompass all areas of your life: emotional, material and spiritual. Create a collage from these on an A4 piece of card or paper and keep it in a prominent place where you will notice it each day. Each time you focus on your collage, consider what you have achieved so far, and ensure that you are open to discovering each new step towards your goal.

Exercise 2. Mapping your route

Take a large sheet of paper, preferably A3. Start in the centre with your goal, and work outwards, noting in capital letters the things that you want to achieve and how you can accomplish this. Add any ideas that will help you or resources that you can call on and draw lines that link these ideas. Write in sub-texts beneath the bold lettering. Use felt-tip coloured pens so that the ideas stand out. Allow yourself to branch out as other ideas come to you.

Exercise 3. Learning levity

View life as a game, with no winners or losers. What makes life a fun experience for you? Do you still play? How often do you allow yourself a belly-laugh, or a moment of silliness? When did you last fly a kite, or play a game of chase? Resolve to release fears of looking silly, and do something that gave you pleasure in the past.

CHAPTER 9

Exercise 1. Focus assessment

What in your life appears to be most "real", solid, and immutable at this moment? Check the energy around this.
Does it feel positive or negative?
Is this "reality" what you wish for in your life?
If so, maintain your focus on it, and allow it to solidify further and become rooted within you.

Exercise 2. The bubble game

Buy a child's bubble-blowing kit. Experiment with the bubbles – have fun. See how large you can make them.
Blow several bubbles in quick succession and see each one as a goal that shines in your life.
As each one pops, imagine yourself attaining that goal.

- Think of the feeling that this attainment would generate in you and focus on holding that feeling after the bubbles have gone.

Printed in Great Britain
by Amazon

16293841R00142